NIKOS A. SALINGAROS

TWELVE LECTURES ON ARCHITECTURE

ALGORITHMIC SUSTAINABLE DESIGN

NOTES FROM A SERIES OF 12 LECTURES
APPLYING CUTTING-EDGE MATHEMATICAL TECHNIQUES
TO ARCHITECTURAL AND URBAN DESIGN.

NIKOS A. SALINGAROS

TWELVE LECTURES ON ARCHITECTURE
— ALGORITHMIC SUSTAINABLE DESIGN —
ISBN 978-3937954-035

CONTENTS

LECTURE 10 : CODES THAT GENERATE LIVING URBAN STRUCTURE.

LECTURE 11 : NEW URBANISM AND TALL BUILDINGS.

LECTURE 12 : CHILDREN, SOCIAL HOUSING,
AND COMPUTING THE CITY.

INTRODUCTION

ALEXANDROS A. LAVDAS

In the early twentieth century, music, like all the arts, went through cataclysmic changes; the very concept of tonality was challenged when a number of composers started experimenting with different atonal systems. Abolishing tonality in music was tantamount to abolishing syntax in language. This is something that every composer knows and, these days, so does every cognitive neuroscientist. Unexpected notes (out of tonality) in a tonal sequence evoke the same reaction in the brain as does the appearance of syntactically wrong words in a sentence, as shown with functional MRI scans. The experiment of atonality was a purely intellectual one; it neither came from nor did it satisfy the emotional parameters that music relates to. Actually, it was not just intellectual, it was more narrowly academic: because music has been loaded with heavy intellectual content *using the language of tonality* for centuries. Atonality sought to destroy the language itself; with the language destroyed, conveying any meaning, intellectual or other, automatically becomes much more difficult.

If this story sounds awfully familiar to an audience interested in architecture, it is for a good reason. The modernist movement, and especially its deconstructivist incarnation, have arisen from the same intellectual processes and have moved towards the same language-destroying targets. There is a difference, however. The atonal movement in music did not totally dominate the twentieth century, although some composers persisted in following it dogmatically. The uncomfortable psychological effect of atonality was recognized not only by those who completely avoided it, but also by composers like Leonard Bernstein who would occasionally use an atonal theme *precisely* for this unsettling effect. Like another color in his music palette.

In architecture, modernism sought to dominate architecture and ostracize all other forms of architectural expression, by pretending it was not a style, but a totally different approach. It has both succeeded and failed in that goal. It has certainly dominated most of the 20th century but, on the other hand, its main ideological weapon — the claim that "form follows function" regardless of the aesthetics achieved — has been proven to be wrong. For modernism created its own aesthetics: Marcel Breuer's *Wassily chair* or Ludwig Mies van der Rohe's *Barcelona chair* are clearly not made in the simplest, most utilitarian manner. Some of us actually find them quite beautiful, and therein lies the ideological failure of modernism. Revealed to be, after all, nothing but just another style, with its good and bad moments, it automatically loses the moral high ground and with it the right to judge all non-modernist art as inferior or degenerate.

Nikos Salingaros argues that the Bauhaus slogan "form follows function" is, in fact a euphemism for the real agenda: "form follows purpose". And the purpose is the religious imposition of modernist principles. Modernism uses technology to implement designs that are the product of an ideology; the system works from the top to the bottom, with technology as the intermediary.

Salingaros moves in the opposite direction. He is using science, not technology, to dissect out the multitude of parameters that have contributed, through a Darwinian selection of sorts, to pre-modernist architecture. He then uses his observations to formulate sets of rules. As a scientist, he could stop there; these rules could be used to facilitate studying the phenomenon of the interaction of the human being with his/her environment. Instead, he takes a step further: he uses the rules to formulate algorithms on which architectural design could be based to achieve optimum results. This may sound restrictive at first; and yet it is not. The "restrictiveness" of the algorithm depends on the complexity of its implementation. In a highly complex application, an algorithm does not give pre-determined results, it just avoids pre-determined errors. And, as the algorithms are based on observations about the interactions between human beings and their environment, this approach is in fact working from the bottom up. Fully aware that buildings are basically meant to serve their inhabitants' needs, he argues that the current architectural situation is the equivalent of a very large-scale experiment on humans. An experiment that is not only inhumane — because it is not biophilic — but also scientifically flawed: for, unlike biomedical experiments, it is conducted without appropriate controls and without any feedback.

Through an elegant analysis, Salingaros shows how the information load, and also the way that this information is ordered and structured, is essential to the biophilic character of a building. There is no wonder why Art Deco, although modern in a sense, is infinitely more interesting than what followed: it simplifies decorative details, it makes them more rigid and geometrical, but it does not abolish them altogether. Some "information load" is lacking on a three-dimensional level, compared to older styles (even to its immediate predecessor Art Nouveau), but it makes up for it, to some extent, by its choice and use of materials such as marble, which is rich in information content on two dimensions.

It seems that modernist buildings in the International Style actually look better when they are viewed on a large scale. A single storey modernist building may have no detail at all in more than one or two scale levels; a 20-storey modernist building might inevitably have more scale levels: the building scale, the storey scale, the window (or lattice of curtain-wall) scale. Structural details will give it some extra scaling, making it more pleasing to the eye than a small building of the same style, for reasons not related to the architect's intentions; however, its lack of ordered scaling and complexity below 2-3 levels makes it, at a glance, much less satisfying to look at than a pre-modernist building. A building such as this lacks scaling coherence and is, in fact, informationally collapsible: all of the building can be reconstructed by simple repetitions of one simple unit. Deconstructivist and postmodern buildings also lack scaling coherence, but for different reasons. Drawing conclusions from biology and elementary particle physics, Salingaros demonstrates how such buildings, in effect, lack "life", which is an emergent property of matter and energy that requires certain degrees of hierarchical complexity.

In an era when often cloudy "new age" approaches are presented as an antidote to mechanization, the work of Nikos Salingaros demonstrates how a new approach is possible through the scientific method: wholism through careful dissection, and then re-application of all the parameters involved.

Trying to follow the arguments of modernist architects often feels like ice-skating: it can be pleasant, but one has the eerie feeling that one's feet are not firmly on the ground. Reading Nikos Salingaros' writings seems to have the opposite effect: readers are reassured that their "gut feeling" should not be frowned upon and ignored, that what one likes and dislikes is not irrelevant, but that it can in fact be systematically analyzed and used for constructing better buildings and a better future for humanity.

AUTHOR'S INTRODUCTION

«Αυτό που με ενδιαφέρει απολύτως — και θα έπρεπε να ενδιαφέρη όλους — είναι ότι η Νέα Πόλις θα ολοκληρωθή, θα γίνη. Όχι βεβαίως από αρχιτέκτωνας και πολεοδόμους οιηματίας, που ασφαλώς πιστεύουν, οι καημένοι, ότι μπορούν αυτοί τους βίους των ανθρώπων εκ των προτέρων να ρυθμίζουν και το μέλλον της ανθρωπότητος, με χάρακες, με υποδεκάμετρα, γωνίες και «ταυ», μέσα στα σχέδια της φιλαυτίας των, ναρκισσευόμενοι (μαρξιστικά, φασιστικά ή αστικά), πνίγοντες και πνιγόμενοι, να κανονίζουν.» — Ανδρέας Εμπειρίκος, «Όχι Μπραζίλια μα Οκτάνα».

"What interests me absolutely — and which should interest everyone — is that the New City will be realized, it will be built. Of course, not by arrogant architects and urbanists, who, stifling and stifled in plans of their own conceit and acting narcissistically (whether in a Marxist, fascist, or bourgeois manner), certainly and pitifully believe that they can arrange people's lives beforehand and regulate the future of humanity using rulers, measurements, triangles, and T-squares." — Andreas Embirikos, "Not Brasilia but Octana".

I'm pleased to present this series of lecture notes to architecture students and young architects. Ever since videotaping a presentation of twelve lectures on my own conception of the theoretical foundations of architecture and urbanism, I have had numerous requests to make the lecture notes available. The reason is that, although the lecture videos are posted freely on the Web, some students around the world with poor internet connections find it difficult to follow them, and would like to have a printed copy of the material in a handy format. I naturally proposed to my editor that these lecture notes be transformed into a proper book, but he discouraged me, saying that: "The notes have a compactness that would be lost if they were replaced by dense theoretical text, and they are much easier to follow now. Anyway, students will learn directly from the explanatory figures." Or perhaps he was afraid that the book would grow to become too thick for the market.

And so I limited myself to inserting explanatory paragraphs throughout the text, wherever those friends who reviewed the lecture notes felt that some additional discussion would be helpful. I listened again to the original video lectures and noted those points where I gave some extemporaneous explanations, and that material is now included in the explanatory paragraphs. On the other hand, as my friend and colleague Kenneth Masden pointed out, each section of every chapter could be expanded into a separate course with additional details and explanation, so for him it's great that so much information is presented here in compact form. Masden feels that the present format gives an opportunity to whoever is teaching a studio or theory course to assign this book and to provide the details, and thus a way to get the instructor involved in interpreting the results.

I am not so optimistic, since most if not all of the material presented here lies outside contemporary architectural education and practice. Architecture lacks a common established tradition of knowledge that would make it easy to correctly interpret my notes. Worse than that, many instructors either teach design rules that are the opposite of those I present in these lectures, or they mistakenly (and arrogantly) believe they already know everything of value, and thus dismiss all of this material as unnecessary. Despite these obstacles, a large number of young people around the world have found in my work an invaluable source for learning about what architecture really is, and also the tools for building the "New City": a living environment on the human scale. In the end, this book will probably find a use for learning outside the present system of architectural education, and that may be its role in shaping the architects of the future.

Architecture and urbanism are formulated here as applications of computations. By applying cutting-edge mathematical techniques to architectural and urban design, a new toolbox is presented to design practitioners. Each step in the design process, on every scale, corresponds to a computation. This series of lectures brings together geometrical constructs such as Cellular Automata, recursive growth, the Fibonacci sequence, fractals, universal scaling, etc. Few of these topics are currently taught in architecture schools, nor are simple descriptions available for non-mathematicians. All of these disparate techniques are woven together into one useful design tool, which can be used by both architecture students and practitioners. The design methodology combines structural rules with a free design/computational method that liberates a designer from any previously held design dogma.

Complex systems and computational reducibility are frameworks that help to formulate the basis for a general theory of design, by understanding the algorithmic complexity of the design process. The theory of intelligence and memory storage is intimately tied to interactive computations. Concepts from biology such as morphogenesis, the evolution of structural features, and embryonic development are applied to architectural and urban design. There are remarkable instances of how these techniques generate natural forms such as plants, seashells, and other organisms, and those can be successfully transferred to create the built environment. Evolutionary regression is also essential in understanding the historical drift of architectural styles. Architectural viruses play an important though negative role by erasing traditional form languages.

Christopher Alexander's most recent work is highlighted and explained with simple examples. The computations necessary for design decisions have to follow a very specific sequence; otherwise the end-result will be dysfunctional. Alexander's classic work on "Pattern Languages" is an essential part of adaptive design, since Alexandrine patterns provide essential constraints on every adaptive computation, without which buildings or urban regions becomes uninhabitable. Results from theoretical physics delve deeply into the concept of symmetry. Using elementary particle symmetries to better understand the process of symmetry breaking reveals how to create "energy" in architecture through the use of ornament. It is shown how indigenous design, such as is practiced in building favelas, bears a striking parallel with the mechanism by which mobile robots function.

On the urban scale, New Urbanist codes should finally replace the post World-War II zoning that created cities fit only for cars. The regeneration of cities and suburbs depends upon the type of urban computations that are described here. Tall buildings come in for severe criticism as not offering any true energy benefit, but many hidden costs: they are neither the solution towards achieving urban density, nor to creating green urban regions. The correct manner to designing a sustainable urban plaza is outlined. In so many cases today, a "sculptural" conception of the city destroys urban life because it is completely foreign to human scale, movement, and interactions. It is time to recognize that much of what is now being built around the world (by prize-winning architects) is dysfunctional and unsustainable. The scientific results presented here clearly differentiate what works from what doesn't.

PREFACE

GEORGE PAPANIKOLAOU

I came away from reading this book especially informed and much more optimistic. This rarely happens these days... I would like to note my personal impressions and all the thoughts that were generated in someone who comes from an entirely different discipline.

Before coming into contact with this book, I would have looked with special mistrust at anybody who claimed that architecture could be ranked among the sciences. Even more so, as the criterion of what constitutes a good and successful design seemed to be lost in labyrinthine conversations among experts. This book reminds us of the obvious starting point that in the final analysis, successful works are those that are used, loved by their residents, and which help them to develop all those activities and emotions that make their users more human. This reflection locates architecture in its true calling, a mission that is deeply human-centered.

We work, we fall in love, we cook, we meet, we communicate, and raise our children (only to mention for example a minimal number of different functions and human needs) within a space that we actively construct and shape, but which in turn shapes us. It either offers us or it removes possibilities. If one thinks about it, this multiplicity of needs that have to be satisfied simultaneously and to coexist harmoniously inside living space is by no means smaller than what we meet in nature, in ecosystems, or in the organization of multi-cellular organisms. Therefore, the magnitude of the challenge posed by architecture and urbanism is not inferior to the other sciences such as the life sciences.

In those sciences, we have finally learned after a series of mistakes, faulty theories and methodologies that complex phenomena cannot be grasped and cannot be explained, nor do they lead to viable applications that come from the ideas of some inspired geniuses. Rather, insight comes from a laborious and collective effort in which everyone collaborates with his/her own building stone in building up the edifice of common knowledge. In the field of genetics, pioneering methods of organizing scientific work through collaboration were applied in the past few decades in an innovative manner, within the framework of a world-wide scientific society using methodologies, algorithmic methods of computation and knowledge sources open to all researchers, with the result that we achieved great and complex works such as reading the human genome. The modern model of a successful scientist in our discipline (and I don't yet include Medicine, which lags with a constant delay) tends to be modest, and to increasingly refer to individuals who managed to organize a collaborative effort with an inspired method. Why should an architect constitute an exception to this?

Work of such complexity as architectural and urban design has to benefit from the methodological achievements of the other sciences. Partitioning the problem into smaller parts, analyzing those parts, creating smaller organized constituents that can be tried out experimentally so that their possible errors can be fixed, the use of basic rules for re-composing the whole again, utilizing human intuition as a subconscious computing resource that incorporates both knowledge and practice, organizing the participation of many partners for the success of complex works that can neither be conceived nor constructed by isolated individuals — these are some of the contemporary practices that this book incorporates into architectural theory.

The city is not simply a human ecosystem but an organized system that has to be made to fit harmonically inside the natural ecosystem if it wishes to be viable. The challenge is great.

The book's criticism of modernism occurs on many levels and is justified. It should not be perceived only as a polemic, but as a tool to show new directions by means of demonstrating the difference with the old (modernist) ones. The difference is in fact significant and systematic and is slowly dawning at the appropriate historical moment. Looking back, architecture and urbanism is only one sphere of the modern age's expressions of misfortunes. Analogies exist in almost all sectors of human endeavor, as for example the catastrophic exhaustion of natural resources and biodiversity. Facing the darkness of the threatened catastrophe, the beginning of a period of arduous re-arrangements, political instability, and growing unhappiness, we can understand as a species how foolishly we have behaved up until now. Is this however enough? No. A German philosopher said that the problem with the world is that we need to change it. In order to do that, we require well-established scientific ideas and practical directions for action. And it is this that makes this book especially integrated. It does not limit itself to reviewing all the basic rules, it does not restrict itself to criticism, but it reminds us of the objective — which is to serve humankind — and it shows us the methodology and organizational forms upon which we can rely in order to try and achieve this goal. This is a virtue that one rarely finds nowadays in a theoretical treatise. It is an invitation towards building a living human ecosystem.

Seldom does one have the good fortune to read an educational book of such clarity and directness. More than that, however, it is an educational book that opens wide the reader's horizons and helps him/her to see the analogies and internal affinities with other sciences, embodying their most important successes into architectural theory. I believe that this book crystallizes a historical necessity (and if it were not written by this author, it would have had to be written sooner or later by someone else). There is a need for architectural theory to be founded once again upon a scientific foundation that will allow it to fulfill its new historical duty: the creation of a new living world. For this reason I believe that this book's ideas will grow stronger in the domain of architecture with the coming years, they will be discussed, and will constitute the embryo for the architecture of the future. Justly, therefore, it is titled "the future of architectural theory". As for its author, he is simply carrying out his historical duty.

As a result of the breadth of its discussion, this book stimulated many thoughts having to do with the historical development of the sciences. I believe that our own sciences also followed a parallel path and discovered their present-day self by following an analogous sequence of steps to those of architecture. I think that the reversal of the presently established situation is unavoidable, and time is on the author's side.

LECTURE 1:
COMPLEXITY AND SCALING.

1.1. RECURSION AND THE FIBONACCI SEQUENCE.

1.2. UNIVERSAL SCALING.

1.3. BIOPHILIA.

1.4. SCALING FROM DIVISION.

1.5. COMBINATORIAL COMPLEXITY.

1.1. RECURSION AND THE FIBONACCI SEQUENCE.

ALGORITHMIC DESIGN

» An algorithm is a set of instructions that can be followed to achieve a desired, but not always pre-determined end result
» Goes through successive states
» Breaks up the problem into smaller steps
» Sometimes uses recursive feedback
» Contrast with a conception of "all at once"

In a simple system, an algorithm computes a result through a sequence of operations, and leads to a straightforward result just like an arithmetic computation in a calculator. In a complex system, however, there could be many related results that satisfy the required conditions, so there is no single unique result. The algorithm in a complex case (for example, architecture) has to break up the problem into smaller steps. This decomposition helps to cut down the choices so as to avoid the infinite number of non-desirable states, and to zero in on the much smaller number of acceptable results. Using some hypothetical numbers, say, we wish to comprehend the complexity of a problem that presents 100,000 possible states and to reach towards the 10 desirable results that are more-or-less optimal.

DESIGN AS COMPUTATION

» We use algorithms to compute a result
» In the absence of an algorithm, we retrieve a result from memory — such computation is therefore based on what is stored in memory
» In architecture, memory of typology influences the results of new designs
» An algorithm makes us independent of memory, hence more creative

SUSTAINABLE DESIGN

» Use morphogenetic rules that nature follows
» Mimic but not copy physical, and especially biological structures
» The limitations of natural materials constrain built forms to certain geometries
» Sticking on a solar panel does not connect to the intrinsic geometry of nature!

A "morphogenetic" rule is a prescription for obtaining a form (from the Greek word morphe) via some sort of genetic information. Working within this approach to design, we seek simple rules that generate complex forms out of many steps rather than having the form specified all at once. This is the way that biology works to build the bodies of living organisms: coded information is applied to assemble chemical elements into a very complex form that is alive.

ARITHMETIC RECURSION

» A repeated operation with feedback
» Fibonacci sequence:
» Start with the number 1, then add 1
» Continue adding the previous two numbers to obtain the infinite sequence
» 1, 1, 2, 3, 5, 8, 13, 21, 34, 55, 89, 144, …

UNIVERSAL SCALING HIERARCHY

» We already have the mathematical tools for a fundamental result in architecture
» **"The alternate terms of the Fibonacci sequence are a check for subdivisions in an adaptive design"**
» {1, 3, 8, 21, 55, 144, 377, 987, 2584, … }

APPLICATIONS TO DESIGN. (I) GOING UP IN SCALE

» Take the smallest built scale, e.g. a step (has to be a certain height because of the size of human beings). Then, the next larger scale should be about 3 times that step, the next largest scale about 8 times the step, the next scale about 21 times the step, the next scale about 55 times, etc., going up to the size of the whole building
» The design should try to avoid significant scales in-between these approximate scales

APPLICATIONS TO DESIGN. (II) GOING DOWN IN SCALE

» Take the largest built scale, e.g. the building or its main feature. The next smaller scale should be about 1/3 of the largest dimension, the next smallest about 1/8 times the largest dimension, the next 1/21 of the largest dimension, etc., going right down to the size of small details
» There should be no significant scales in-between these scales

The universal scaling rule aids us in making architectural design decisions such as "should I make this particular building component 1m or 5m large?" By checking the existing smaller and larger components that are fixed by human physiology or by other constraints on size, our decision is made much easier. This is not meant to be a straitjacket for design, as the rule is only approximate, nor does it dictate the formal geometry (unlike the modernist design vocabulary, which certainly does dictate actual forms). If the designer has complete freedom to make elements of a building at any size, then universal scaling helps to cut down the number of possibilities and to make the design process more efficient. It also helps to make the building more harmonious, and to recover the often-neglected smaller scales from 2m down to 5mm.

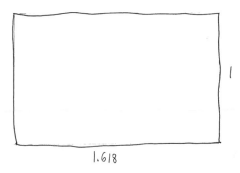

The Golden Rectangle, where 1.618 = (1+√5)/2

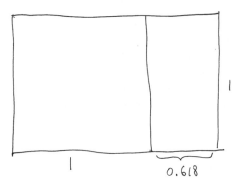

Subdividing into a square plus a vertical golden rectangle

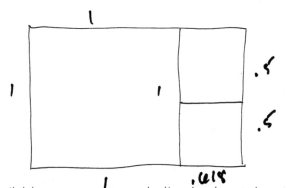

Two subdivisions generate a similar horizontal rectangle: two golden rectangles in the same direction

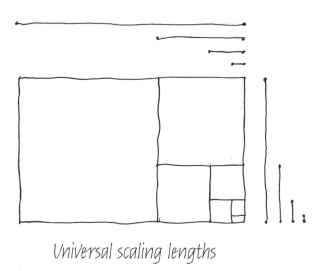

Universal scaling lengths

We thus generate two sequences of lengths: vertical dimensions as sides of golden rectangles, and horizontal dimensions also as sides of golden rectangles. Both sequences separately obey the universal scaling introduced above (very approximately, because the numbers we get from the golden rectangles are not the same as the scaling sequence). Nevertheless, an architect who wishes to understand universal scaling but doesn't know the Fibonacci sequence can just look at the golden rectangles and see the relative ratios between successive scales in a building that lead to design coherence. This picture also shows how we continue into smaller and smaller scales.

MATHEMATICAL SCALING RATIO

» The limit of the ratio of alternate terms of the Fibonacci sequence as the terms get large is a fixed irrational number, 2.618 = 1 + Golden Mean Φ
» Powers of 2.618 do not exactly give the integers 3, 8, 21, 55, etc. because the Fibonacci sequence is not a geometric sequence.

THE EXPONENTIAL SEQUENCE: ANOTHER TOOL FOR UNIVERSAL SCALING

» Practical tool: use a geometric sequence of powers of the logarithmic constant $e = 2.72$, which determines the shape of animal horns, shells, etc.
» 1, $e = 2.72$, $e^2 = 7.39$, $e^3 = 20.1$, $e^4 = 54.6$, $e^5 = 148$
» This geometric sequence is approximately equal to the universal scaling sequence, and is certainly close enough to compute the scaling ratios for generating architectural subdivisions.

1.2. UNIVERSAL SCALING.

CONSTRAINTS

» Constraints make design easier by narrowing down choices
» There are several constraints that guide design to adapt towards innate (biologically-based) human sensibilities
» Universal scaling is a necessary but not sufficient condition for adaptive design

----

A constraint is a rule that specifies either an exact condition to be satisfied, or a range of parameters within which a result must occur. For example, an architectural constraint could be "the buildings has to be 17.4 meters high", or possibly "the width of the sidewalk can be anywhere from 1.2 m to 2.4 m, but no narrower and no wider". I propose a very general constraint to apply to all structures, on an architectural scale as well as an urban scale. This constraint does not refer to specific dimensions or measurements, but instead to a scaling relationship among ALL dimensions present in the design. The constraint of universal scaling applies to the approximate ratio between any two successive scales as defined by the components of a structure. This constraint is meant to apply independently to the lengths and widths of built components, and I claim that a design is better adapted to human sensibilities if it satisfies this constraint.

UNIVERSAL SCALING HIERARCHY

» Extends the old "Rule of 3" used in the past, by giving all the other terms
» See "A Theory of Architecture", Umbau-Verlag, Solingen, Germany, 2006: Chapters 2 & 3.
» Develops earlier results by Christopher Alexander in "The Nature of Order, Book 1", Center for Environmental Structure, Berkeley, California, 2001.

The "Rule of 3" is sometimes found in historical (ancient or medieval) building manuals in statements such as this: "make sure that there is something three times what you are building, and also something that is one-third the size of what you are building". I am referring to a rule of thumb that has long ago dropped out of the common architectural conscience. In truth, nothing like this survived into the twentieth century, so several generations of architects have no knowledge of it.

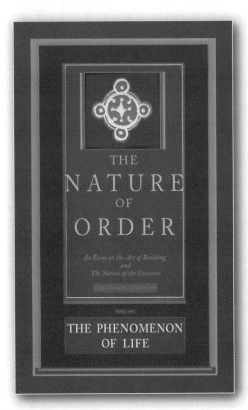

Christopher Alexander's „The Nature of Order, Book I"

„A Theory of Architecture"

THE GOLDEN MEAN

» It so happens that universal scaling is related to the square of the golden mean Φ
» $\Phi^2 = \Phi + 1 = 2.618$
» This interesting coincidence has nothing to do with the proportions of rectangles, such as credit cards, the carefully-chosen front elevation of the Parthenon, and other buildings!

Note *an essential difference in our approach: the Golden Mean is traditionally applied to rectangles, whereas here I'm talking about a sequence of lengths that have nothing particularly to do with rectangles. In a rectangle, one compares its width with its length, which is irrelevant for universal scaling; I measure dimensions of architectural components in the same direction, and compute the relative ratios between successive scales. In addition, many of the famous examples of the Golden Mean to architecture have to be carefully chosen to come out right (does one include the Parthenon's triangular pediment and the steps or not?).*

ARCHITECTURES THAT OBEY UNIVERSAL SCALING

» Gothic Architecture
» Classical Western Architecture
» Islamic Architecture
» Vernacular architectures the world over
» Traditional architectures from all cultures and all periods
» NOT international modernism

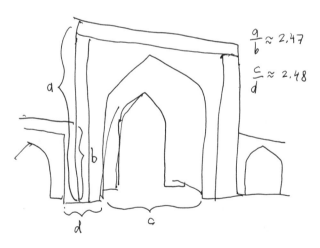

$$\frac{a}{b} \approx 2.47$$

$$\frac{c}{d} \approx 2.48$$

Masjid-i-Shah, Isfahan

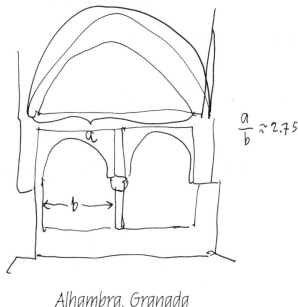

$$\frac{a}{b} \approx 2.75$$

Alhambra, Granada

VALIDATION FROM EVOLUTION

» All the cultures we know evolved universal scaling in their indigenous architectures, both vernacular and monumental
» Universal scaling is therefore innate
» The exceptions are military fortifications and the Pyramids, which had to appear unapproachable from the outside

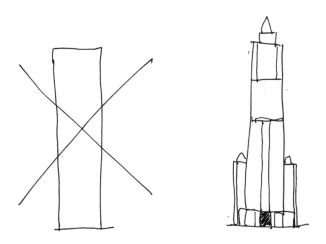

Application to skyscrapers: the glass-and-steel box versus an early Art-Deco skyscraper

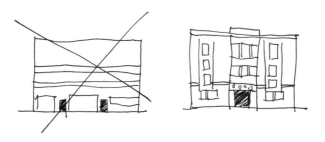

Application to house façades: two residential buildings of similar size, Modernist versus Art Deco

THE SMALLER SCALES

» The comparison we just did with two residences of roughly the same size and shape is seen on only the larger scales
» But it is on the smaller scales that the difference is really dramatic
» In the modernist house, there are no smaller scales, thus no scaling hierarchy

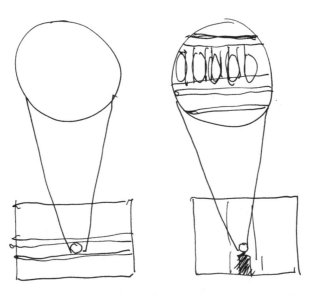

Magnification reveals the smaller scales, or their absence, in the two residential buildings shown above

I'm giving out a challenge by claiming that the vast majority of buildings all around the world before the industrial age obey universal scaling (and actually continuing into the early industrial years). This holds for all different cultures, all different periods, and is not restricted to a few carefully-selected buildings that I might refer to here. This claim can be documented by on-site measurements, and then the term "universal" becomes apparent, since it applies *to indigenous architectures, both vernacular and monumental. Universal scaling is therefore innate to how human beings create forms, and is not a feature tied to any particular culture.*

APPLICATION: WIDE BOUNDARIES

»   An articulation needs its edge defined
»   Commensurate with universal scaling, edges or centers should have a lip
»   This gives us wide door and window frames, baseboards, pilasters
»   There is no longer a need to show off industrial materials without supports

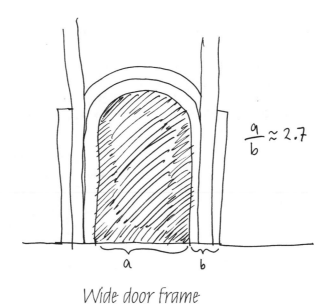

$$\frac{a}{b} \approx 2.7$$

Wide door frame

Frames were eliminated in the 20th Century to show off the strength of new industrial materials: a door or window no longer needed a thick structural frame for strengthening. This was taken to the extreme of bringing the wall right up to the opening and smoothing out the transition, soon becoming a fetish in a minimalist expression of a door or window as a hole-in-the-wall. Few people realize that the dominant form language in use today is just a statement of bravura that has long outlived its psychologically shocking message. On the contrary, a user gets a sense of coherence and stability when confronted with a thick boundary to an opening.

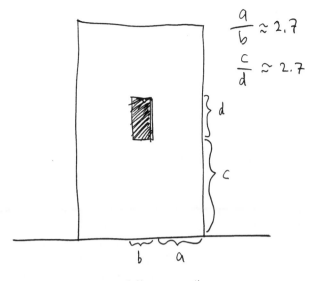

$$\frac{a}{b} \approx 2.7$$

$$\frac{c}{d} \approx 2.7$$

Center follows scaling

SUMMARY

» Use ratios of lengths to aid design
» Change in thinking about "proportion"
» NOT the ratio of the sides of a rectangle, but compare instead dimensions of objects measured along the same direction
» Nothing magical or mystical about this

1.3. BIOPHILIA.

WHAT IS BIOPHILIA?

» Edward O. Wilson used the term to describe an innate connection between all living beings
» More specifically, human beings have a biologically-founded link to other life-forms
» The connection is genetic — it resides in the common parts of our DNA

HUMAN SENSORY SYSTEMS

» Have evolved to respond to natural geometries of fractals, colors, scaling, symmetries
» Fine-tuned to perceive positive aspects (food, friends, mates) and threats

» Also fine-tuned to detect pathologies of our body, signaled by the departure from natural geometries

BIOPHILIA AND HEALTH

» Human beings require contact with the geometry of biological structures
» Experiments in hospitals show much faster post-operative healing in rooms looking out at trees
» Social and mental health deteriorates in nature-less surroundings

We are experiencing a re-discovery of fundamental truths that people knew intrinsically in traditional cultures. We seek knowledge of how to design living environments that make us healthier. An overwhelming amount of experimental evidence has proved the biophilic effect, with more data added every day. These experiments crucial to our health and wellbeing are of little interest to architects, who continue to implement their iconic image-based projects. The experiments themselves are carried out by scientists and by researchers in the medical profession. Biophilia as a discipline comes out of biology and ecology. I continue to wonder how architects can live and work in a world totally isolated from human beings and human physiology, yet continue to receive commissions and win architectural prizes.

HEALTHY ENVIRONMENTS

» A healthy mind in a healthy body — which is situated in a healthy environment!
» Positive emotional response to the environment reduces stress and thus raises resistance to disease (external & internal)
» Emotional regeneration: the feelings inside a great Mosque, Cathedral, or Temple

My former student Yannick Joye is investigating the notion of biophilia as a healing effect of the perception of forms, as a set of restorative responses. The essence of the argument is that restoration (i.e. stress-reduction and attention restoration) is the result of easy perceptual processing because certain forms resonate with our own physiological make-up. Biophilic architecture is thus composed of forms, volumes, and surfaces that are processed by the neuroperceptive system as fluently as are natural, living forms. This would explain their conjectured restorative effects. Several researchers are ready to test these effects is laboratory experiments.

- » Traditional architects use universal scaling intuitively, but very few people can get this kind of training today
- » One exception: the memory of Classical architectural typologies is enough to guide the designer doing a traditional Classical building today
- » The problem is with design outside a traditional form language

....

In conclusion, we need to develop constraints to make adaptive design easier by narrowing down choices. Human beings have in their genetic, perceptual, and biological structure an innate set of rules to adapt to their environments. We need to discover several distinct sets of rules that guide us towards adaptive design. One of these is the universal scaling. At the end of these lectures, we will possess a list of conditions that, if satisfied, will lead us to adaptive design. That knowledge will enable us to validate traditional form languages so that they can be used again today without being condemned as "old-fashioned". We will also set up criteria with which to create new innovative form languages.

....

1.4. SCALING FROM DIVISION.

ORIGINS OF SCALING

- » A larger form can be virtually divided into smaller parts
- » Division generates the smaller scales
- » Grouping of smaller elements occurs within larger scale
- » Similarity establishes scaling coherence among distinct scales

ANALOGY WITH EMBRYONIC DEVELOPMENT

- » The embryo starts out as a single cell
- » It subdivides into an increasing number of cells, clustering into groups
- » All the subsequent cell divisions work together to form the growing embryo
- » Insights of Christopher Alexander

DIVISION IN ONE DIMENSION

- » To illustrate scale formation through division, consider only lengths
- » One-dimensional architectural model makes computations easier
- » Divide a length into 2, 3, or more parts of comparable size

HOW MANY DIVISIONS?

» Smaller scales are created by subdividing the larger scale
» Simplest division is into two parts
» Too many identical parts, however, produce combinatorial complexity

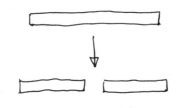

Divide into two identical parts

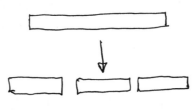

Divide length into 3 parts

RECOMBINATION

» The parts created by division must be appropriate for reconstructing the original larger scale
» Division as a process that reinforces, and does not destroy, the whole
» Grouping and recombination relates daughter and parent scales

LINKING SCALES

» Scaling hierarchy grows out of a relationship among three scales:
» A particular scale that
» — generates an immediately smaller scale through division
» — and is related to its immediately larger scale through grouping

THE GOLDEN MEAN DOESN'T APPLY!

» It is impossible to divide a form into fewer than 2 comparable parts
» Therefore, we cannot use a scaling factor of $\Phi = 1.618$ to divide a form
» This elementary error was made by Le Corbusier in proposing his Modulor scheme for design

Relationship of 1.62 : 1

CONCLUSION: THE SCALING FACTOR

» Scaling from division defines the lowest value for the scaling factor
» The scaling factor must be larger than or equal to 2
» — but not so large that we face the problem of combinatorial complexity

1.5. COMBINATORIAL COMPLEXITY.

» Monotonous repetition is a problem
» Suppose we have a large number of identical smaller parts
» Triggers comparison, a combinatorial process that generates fatigue
» Monotonous repetition is thus not only boring, it can actually be stressful

UNEXPECTED COMPLEXITY

» NOT Kolmogorov complexity, which considers monotonous repetition as simple instead of complex
» — measures complexity as the length of the algorithm required to produce it
» We are instead interested in a very different combinatorial complexity

NEURAL SYSTEM

» Evolved to cope with the natural world
» Expends energy to arrange data from senses into coherent patterns
» Tries to group similar pieces into larger wholes (Gestalt)
» Keeps working to find some grouping

CONJECTURE ON PERCEPTION

» The brain works combinatorially
» Tries out all possible geometric combinations, deciding which is more effective for understanding
» In the absence of explicit groupings, this process leads to stress and fatigue

COGNITIVE STRESS

» Repeating parts are actually perceived as interacting
» Combinatorial complexity increases with the number of identical parts
» Solution is to iteratively partition sets of parts into coherent groups

I claim that a simple repetition, which Kolmogorov complexity defines as having low complexity, is no longer perceived as simple when the number of repeating parts becomes large. The reasons are unclear but probably have to do with a set of objects perceived as interacting, a result of how our cognitive system is constructed. Human beings do not automatically count sequentially — we usually grasp the whole configuration almost instantaneously, and interpret it on different scales simultaneously. We have to be taught as children to count repeating parts, but children already have very advanced spatial cognitive skills that rely upon grouping and symmetries.

MONOTONOUS REPETITION IS TIRING

» According to our conjecture, repetition of identical parts is cognitively exhausting
» Need to break the monotony:
» (A) either make each similar part slightly different using variety
» (B) or group the parts into clusters

FIRST SOLUTION: SYMMETRY WITH VARIETY

» Different capitals or surface design on Medieval columns
» Variations in a row of repeating windows, but still in strict alignment
» Repeating units are distinguished by variety on a lower scale

Columns with variety, spaced symmetrically

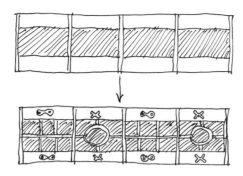

Windows gain variety from smaller scale insertions

SECOND SOLUTION: GROUPING PARTS

» Create intermediate clusters into which several parts assemble into groups
» Grouping generates intermediate scales
» The process of grouping according to scales recursively generates the universal scaling hierarchy

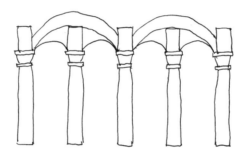

Grouping columns into clusters of three

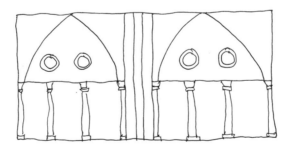

Grouping columns into clusters of four

CREATION OF SCALES

» Solving the combinatorial complexity problem generates the scaling hierarchy
» VARIETY acts on a smaller scale, thus differentiation creates several smaller scales
» GROUPING PARTS creates a larger scale
» But monotonous repetition prevents the formation of the scaling hierarchy

Monotonous repetition is so widespread in industrial and post-industrial design that we need to recognize its purpose, which is to erase and prevent the natural scaling hierarchy. Repetition without any intermediate groupings or symmetries defines just two scales: that of the repeating unit, and the largest scale of the whole ensemble. Simplistic repetition eliminates all intermediate scales. This is, in fact, an unwritten rule of modernist design and planning, taught and propagated through a multitude of examples that do a very efficient job of spreading the method.

LECTURE 2:
FRACTALS AND GRAVITY.

2.1. GEOMETRIC RECURSION AND FRACTALS: THE SIERPINSKI GASKET

ALGORITHM FOR GENERATING THE SIERPINSKI GASKET

» Start with an equilateral triangle
» Subdivide its sides into 1/2, and draw 3 triangles inside the original triangle
» Now subdivide those smaller triangles into 1/2, and repeat the process
» Geometric Recursion

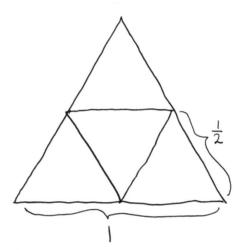

Sierpinski gasket (first iteration)

Here, three similar triangles are facing up, each is 1/2 the size of the original large triangle. Now subdivide those three upwards-pointing triangles in the corners in the same way. A mathematical fractal will have subdivisions going down all the way to infinitesimal scales, but I'm going to stop the division process after only 3 steps. Look at any book on fractals to see how more iterations create a perforated and crinkly structure. When I finish the iterations, I will cut out all the down-pointing triangles, and this perforation creates a "gasket". Note that the subdivisions occur in particular regions, and not all over.

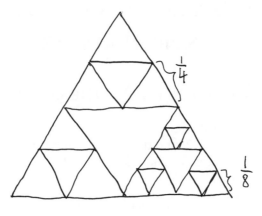

Sierpinski gasket (cont.)

Cut out down-pointing triangles

MATHEMATICAL, NATURAL, AND ARCHITECTURAL FRACTALS

» The Sierpinski gasket is an exact fractal with an infinite number of decreasing scales
» Its scaling factor is 2, not 2.72, so it does not precisely follow universal scaling
» Triangles are a very specific geometry — we are not proposing triangles for the shape of buildings or cities

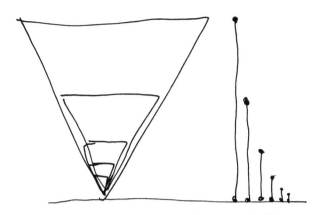

Downward-pointing triangles of Sierpinski gasket show scaling by factor of 2

TWO TYPES OF FRACTALS

» All fractals depart from uniformity
» PERFORATED fractals cut out smaller and smaller pieces (gaskets, sponges, sieves)
» ACCRETIVE fractals add smaller and smaller pieces to build up fine structure (like coral and rivers)

3-D ACCRETIVE FRACTAL CASTLE

» Start with a thick square slab
» Add four smaller square slabs on top of the corners
» Repeat on smaller scales (scaling factor 3) to get castle with turrets

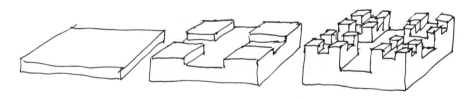

3-D accretive fractal castle

SCALING SYMMETRY CREATES COHERENCE

» Similar shape when a fractal's particular details are magnified
» The brain handles more information encoded in a fractal than if random
» Key to fractal complexity is information compression
» Fractals in nature have similar but not identical features under magnification

The meaning of patterns is that the information presented to us can be compressed. A random array of letters has no meaning for us, but if they convey a pattern of linguistic representation, we can grasp their information. Because of the symmetries and scaling that occurs in fractals, the human brain doesn't have to encode all the distinct scales of such complex structures. Mathematical fractals repeat the same shape on different scales. This idea finds an extremely successful application in fractal compression programs for computer graphics. These work ideally to compress natural scenery, animals, human faces, etc., because those obey fractal scaling to a large extent.

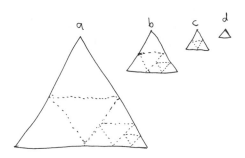

Exact self-similarity in the Sierpinski gasket

PHYSIOLOGICAL WELLBEING

» Self-similarity endows visual coherence — important to human perception
» The brain evolved to handle self-similar natural structures
» We react with alarm at structures that exhibit no scaling coherence

Scaling coherence occurs where there is self-similarity between smaller scales and the larger scale. Not only must several distinct scales be present, but also the scales must be well-defined and obey approximate self-similarity akin to the Universal Scaling. This process links the small scales to the larger scales to create a coherent whole. Natural environments have scaling coherence. For example, a tree has approximate scaling coherence from the details of its leaves to the overall size of the tree. The best architectural environments also have this scaling coherence.

FRACTALS IN ARCHITECTURE 1

» The Cosmati family of mosaicists and floor builders created a series of Sierpinski pavements in 12-14C Italian churches
» African villages have naturally fractal plans, not triangular but circular
» Islamic tile patterns are intrinsically fractal, showing high degree of self-similarity

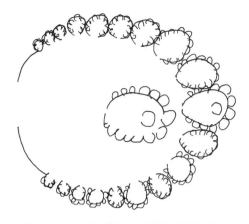

Plan of Ba-ila, Zambia (documented by Ron Eglash)

All architectural and urban scales contribute to coherence. This requires a fractal structure that will link all scales together as much as possible. The smallest scales, as for example tiles in Islamic architecture, are not irrelevant decoration, but play an essential role in establishing the smallest scale of a hierarchical fractal structure. The mathematician Ron Eglash recognized a very rich tradition in African urbanism, architecture, and ornamentation, which was previously dismissed as "not modern". The incredible mathematical sophistication in the shape of African villages was simply not seen, because Western arrogance misinterpreted it as an inability to create exact rectangular plans! Still unappreciated, fractal vernacular architectures are now becoming extinct just like the Siberian Tiger, the Polar Bear, and the Rhinoceros.

Ethiopian silver cross

WESTERN ARROGANCE!

» We can learn from vernacular architecture
» Unfortunately, the West exports non-adaptive, absurd design styles and ty-pologies tied to industrialization
» These erase sustainable local traditions
» Massive media coverage in league with globalization convinces the rest of the world to abandon their culture of building

FRACTALS IN ARCHITECTURE 2

» Manueline Portuguese architecture consists of accretive fractals
» Smallest details are most effectively used on regions closest to users
» Structural information is never wasted — zoom into the area of detail
» Sometimes detail is distributed all over — Hindu temples with sculptures

Detail focused in small region

MINIMALIST MODERNISM IS NOT FRACTAL!

» Only the largest scales are defined
» Maybe one or two scales are present — enormous gap between scales
» No intermediate scales to tie the form together according to universal scaling
» No scaling coherence

POSTMODERNIST & DECONSTRUCTIVIST BUILDINGS ARE NOT FRACTAL

» Opposite problem of minimalist style
» Too many things going on in too many different scales — no scaling hierarchy
» Scale of free-flowing forms is ambiguous
» Nothing is self-similar, because designs deliberately avoid symmetries
» No scaling coherence

» The human body has a hierarchy of scales, from 2 meters down to 1 mm
» Adaptation to human use and senses generates substructures and details and scaling coherence on the human range of scales
» Adaptive buildings connect through a scaling hierarchy to the microscopic structure of the natural materials

$A\!s$ *an example, let's use some hypothetical measurements (rounded out) obtained from the universal scaling hierarchy: 1 mm, 3 mm, 8 mm, 2 cm, 6 cm, 14 cm, 38 cm, 1 m, 2.6 m, etc. These correspond to the human scale. I am not saying that these exact numbers should be used in a particular design: but rather that the ratios among them are correct. Architects at the end of the 19th Century used mass production to incorporate a scaling hierarchy into their architecture through ornamental details. Some examples are Louis Sullivan, Frank Lloyd Wright, Hector Guimard, and Victor Horta. Therefore, this is not a question of natural versus industrial materials, but rather a deliberate choice of a peculiar and narrow style — the imposition of the "machine aesthetic" which is anti-fractal. One can use the cheapest industrial materials with the rules presented here to mimic in a fundamental manner the qualities of more expensive natural materials.*

2.2. PERFORATION, BENDING, AND FOLDING

PROCESS NECESSARY FOR SCALING HIERARCHY

» Morphogenetic development in architecture
» Architectonic elements necessary to define a scaling hierarchy
» Physical model helps to visualize how fractals are generated by stresses

I *wish to visualize how a complex form grows out of more simple forms by using a simple rule (or combination of simple rules). One such process is fractal subdivision, which is explained here. Rather than imagining a form or design that arrives ready-made out of divine inspiration, a complex form develops by stages, using general rules that are themselves rather simple. It is the repeated application of those rules that eventually generates a very complex but at the same time coherent form. One advantage of this fractal approach to design is that it helps to understand natural weathering. A separate and major topic of its own, weathering has been misunderstood by architects in the twentieth century, who have tried in vain to eliminate it. Older architects understood the geometry of the weathering process, and turned it towards reinforcing their design by using fractal scaling in their buildings.*

THREE PROCESSES

» PERFORATION: windows, doors, arcades
» BENDING: departing from straight lines creates structure on smaller scales
» FOLDING: crenellation, pilasters, fluting on columns

PERFORATION: SEMI-PERMEABILITY

» In adaptive architecture, biology, and urbanism, boundaries are not absolute
» Semi-permeable membranes let something through while keeping other things out
» Arcades & bollards: let people through while keeping cars out
» Window grille or Mashrabiya: lets air and light through while keeping people hidden in traditional Islamic architecture (you can look out, but someone in the street cannot see inside because of the light conditions)

Perforation: arcade

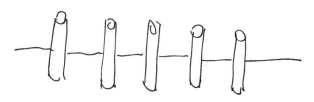

Perforation: bollards

The examples I'm talking about are a thing of the past. Contemporary architects absolutely refuse to use arcades and bollards, so we have to pay a lot of money to go to historic cities to see great examples of urban architecture. Unfortunately, those historic cities are fast replacing their perforated structures with non-perforated modernist western smooth interfaces, in a mad rush towards supposed modernization. In the USA, fire codes forbid the construction of arcades: another example of regulations running amok to make building living urban fabric illegal! Bologna, a city of arcades, has never faced an increased problem from fires during its several centuries of existence.

THE "PUSH-PULL" MODEL — PULL

» Pulling uniformly along a line breaks it at regular intervals (sealing wax on rubber band or sheet)
» Tension generates perforations — gaps on smaller scale
» Eventually leaves only points
» Examples: colonnades, arcades, monumental axis outside Egyptian temples

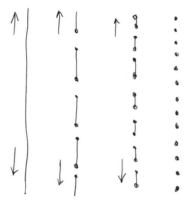

Tension perforates; eventually separates line into points

HORIZONTAL TENSION

» Pulling first separates smooth wall into mostly vertical window and door openings
» Uniform lateral tension separates wall into sections with vertical cuts — arcades
» Further tension separates all wall pieces into columns — creating a straight colonnade
» (This model questions curved colonnades)

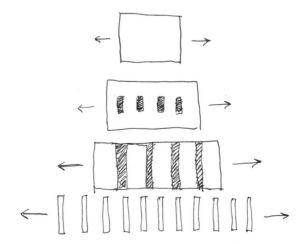

Horizontal tension subdivides plastic material

THE "PUSH-PULL" MODEL — PUSH

» Push a line along its axis so that it folds uniformly
» Generates meanders — new fractal scale
» Compression will eventually bend the whole line to create a curve
» Examples: Circus at Bath; circular plazas surrounded by coffee tables and café alcoves; temple interiors with niches

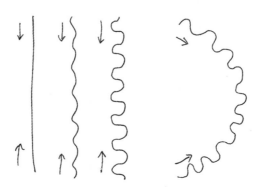

Compression creates meanders, then overall curve

HORIZONTAL COMPRESSION

» Generates smaller structures
» Folding occurs along lines orthogonal to the direction of compression
» Pilasters, thick door and window frames, ceiling beams
» Departure from smooth, straight wall or ceiling

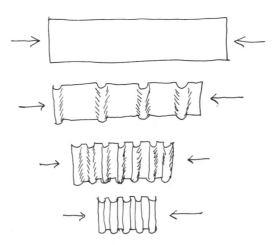

Horizontal compression folds

FOLDING: SPACE-FILLING

» Folding a line is the first step to filling the space slightly
» Meanders create articulations on new, smaller scales
» The boundary of successful urban space needs those smaller scales — which accommodate human activity nodes

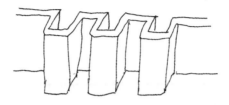

Folding: walls

Fluting on column drum is folding along the circumference

BENDING A SHEET ADAPTS TO VOLUME

» Bending creates a boundary for space
» Domes are best for ceilings, giving the most positive sense of psychological enclosure
» Domes are also more structurally stable
» Urban space needs semi-enclosure on its perimeter, achieved by the surrounding building façades

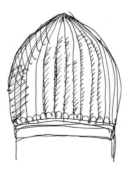

Folding on dome on two distinct scales and directions: folding upwards to form dome and separate fluting around circumference

IMPLICATIONS OF VERTICAL PUSH

» Vertical compression creates folding
» Folding creates horizontal bulges, thick lips
» There are no horizontal gaps, since those would be generated by vertical tension
» No natural mechanism for vertical tension!
» Buildings that show horizontal gaps are perceived as unnatural, and create anxiety

There is nothing in our physiology that prepares us for observing vertical forces directed upwards: that is, something being stretched by being pulled upwards by its top end. Our evolution has taught us to observe natural processes that can push or pull things horizontally, and gravity that pulls and stretches things downwards, but nothing before the industrial age ever pulled upwards. Therefore, even though we are physically capable of implementing structures with vertical tension, we are at a loss to interpret forms that express upward vertical forces. They therefore cause anxiety. I will argue that certain architects achieved notoriety precisely by means of generating vertical anxiety.

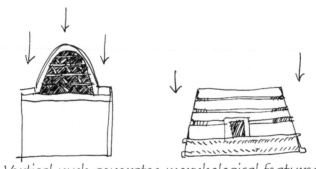

Vertical push generates morphological features

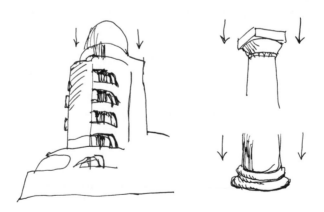

Gravity influences curvature, thickens capitals and bases

The *Einstein observatory by Erich Mendelsohn is molded by gravity "pull-ing" the form down in an elegant manner. A classical column base is just a thickened lip that is the result of "pushing" a column down. The same is true for its capital. A column is therefore an example of the push-pull model. This mechanism can act only in specific directions, however, because of our physiology. The balance mechanism in the inner ear attaches us to the gravitational axis and to its downward direction. Applying the push-pull model in the wrong direction goes against our physiology.*

BIOPHILIC CONSTRAINTS ON THE "PUSH-PULL" MODEL

» Human physiological sensors orient us with the vertical and horizontal axes
» Diagonals generate distress, except when symmetry creates an implicit vertical axis
» BOTH PUSH OR PULL CAN ACT HORIZONTALLY
» Because we evolved with gravity, ONLY PUSH CAN ACT VERTICALLY!

2.3. ANTI-GRAVITY ANXIETY

BUILDING THE UNNATURAL

» Anti-gravity pulls building upwards
» Vertical tension breaks façade, cutting it and separating it into horizontal windows
» Pull creates horizontal gaps and slits between horizontal slabs
» Vertical tension can pull entire building off the ground — maintained by minimal supports (not columns, but stretched pilotis)

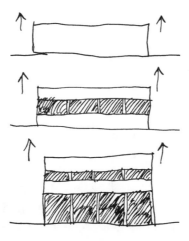

Anti-gravity design pulls building upwards, stretching it upwards, finally breaking it and leaving a horizontal gap.

NOT ROOTED TO THE EARTH

- » Vertical pull lifts building up, like a space ship taking off
- » Building pulls away from humanity
- » Something alien — appears to want to detach from life on earth
- » Columns are the opposite of pilotis

PILOTIS ARE STRETCHED CYLINDERS

- » Pull cylinder uniformly
- » If it is elastic, it will stretch
- » Cylinder will also narrow in diameter

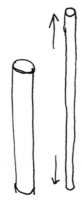

Pilotis are cylinders stretched upwards

COLUMNS ARE COMPRESSED CYLINDERS

- » Push cylinder to create column
- » Pressure widens capital and base
- » Further pressure can buckle column
- » Becomes serpentine column

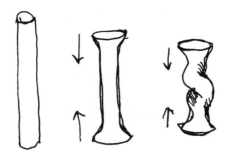

Columns are compressed cylinders

PERVERSE APPLICATION OF "PULL"

- » Universally applied to world architecture
- » Consistent misapplication of our "pull" rule
- » Stretching creates horizontal gaps on many different scales — sometimes fractal?
- » BUT IN THE ONLY DIRECTION THAT CAUSES ANXIETY — VERTICAL

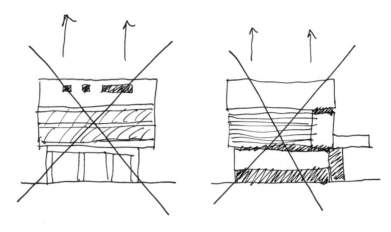

Anti-gravity generates anxiety

POVERTY OF CONCEPTION

- » Some vertical "pull" designs show subdivisions on smaller scales
- » But vertical "pull" buildings are mathematically one-dimensional
- » Any fractal structure is 1-D, because subdivisions are only in one dimension

2.4. ARCHITECTURE OF THE HORIZONTAL

SUPPRESS VERTICAL DIMENSION

- » The British philosopher Roger Scruton first described this idea in a 1980 BBC talk (reprinted in "The Classical Vernacular")
- » This method kills design on the vertical dimension, by simply moving the plan up
- » Buildings become stacks of horizontal slabs
- » The "Domino" house by Le Corbusier

There is something profoundly disturbing about buildings that consist of horizontal slabs. We can understand this physiological/psychological reaction because of anti-gravity anxiety. A large number of horizontal buildings have been built around the world, their architects ignoring our negative reaction to them. In addition to affecting our senses, this method kills architectural design in three dimensions, since building façades cannot be created within this narrow design paradigm. Le Corbusier patented this system, and then propagandized it in his advertising magazine L'Esprit Nouveau. Most people don't know that Le Corbusier for many years made no income from architecture, but earned money from selling advertising in his magazine — he was an advertising pioneer!

ABSURD DESIGN IDEA

» "The plan is the generator" — Le Corbusier writing in his propaganda pamphlet "Towards a New Architecture"
» Draw a ground plan, then translate it upwards to define the building's volume
» Design method taught in all architecture schools today

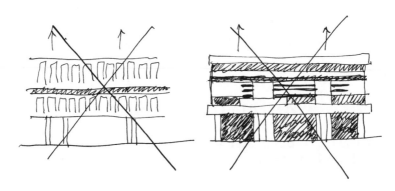

Vertical „pull" design has become the world standard

END OF 3-D DESIGN

» Lifting ground plan to define building eliminates 3-D design altogether
» No façade for human beings to be able to relate to — no adaptivity to senses
» Reduces architecture to 2-D, and to just the ground dimensions (the plan) that are not directly perceivable!
» Spaces in actual building are not designed!

MULTI-STOREY PARKING GARAGES

» Lend themselves to horizontal slab typology
» Anti-gravity anxiety is one reason why they destroy the urban fabric

- » Solution: surround them with real façades
- » Older parking garages in the 1920s had stores on ground floor, and fronting the street on all sides

VENETIAN BLINDS

- » All details contribute either towards anxiety or wellbeing in the built environment
- » Illustration of anti-gravity anxiety from minor elements such as window shades!
- » Venetian blinds fit into windows that are wider horizontally — anxiety
- » Older louvres were embedded into vertical frames — pleasing

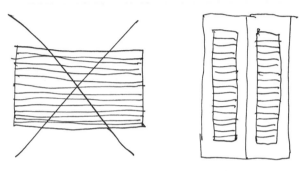

Anxiety-inducing horizontals enclosed by vertical frame to give positive vertical effect

GARAGES IN SUBURBIA

- » The garage opening is a huge horizontal gap
- » Widespread architectural typology, most prominent feature of today's house façades
- » Contributes to dead feeling of suburbia
- » No attempt made to frame a garage opening or to provide a canopy or roof, which would improve the design

Suburbia's principal visual effect is one of horizontal garages, since the garages are the most obvious feature of suburban houses. Front doors are certainly eclipsed by the size of front-opening garages. Again, it was Le Corbusier who first gave prominence to front-opening garages, letting them take over a house's façade. Suburbia is not constituted of stacked horizontal slabs, but it consists of hundreds of garages that contribute to the deadening feeling of that environment. In traditional architectures, structures used for coaches had canopies and columns, and these more human typologies were carried through for a brief period after the introduction of the first automobiles.

CONCLUSION: TYPOLOGIES THAT INDUCE ANXIETY

» Many building and urban typologies that induce anxiety in the viewer were introduced in the early 20th century
» Those typologies have become standardized
» Standardized typologies are copied without even thinking about their consequences
» Our built environment has become deadening and we don't realize why

LECTURE 3:
SMALLER COMPONENTS
AND SUSTAINABILITY.

3.1. UNIVERSAL DISTRIBUTION OF SIZES

3.2. FRACTAL DESIGN, ORNAMENT, AND BIOPHILIA

3.3. SUSTAINABLE SYSTEMS

3.1. UNIVERSAL DISTRIBUTION OF SIZES

A COLLECTION OF SIZES

» Although different from UNIVERSAL SCALING, both concepts are related through fractals
» Count how many components there are in a complex system, according to their relative size — defines a distribution
» All components work together to optimize the system's function

CORRECT DISTRIBUTION HELPS SYSTEMIC STABILITY

» Surprising result for most people:
» The stability of a system depends upon the relative numbers and the distribution of sizes of its components
» Stability also depends on other factors such as system interconnectivity on the same level, and among different levels

COMMON FEATURES

» Universal distribution = inverse-power law (i.e. few large pieces, some intermediate-size pieces, many smaller pieces)
» Central quality that contributes towards sustainability in ecosystems
» Contributes stability to artificial complex systems

UNIVERSAL DISTRIBUTION

» An enormous number of natural and artificial complex systems obey an inverse-power law distribution
» Invertebrate nervous systems, mammalian lungs, DNA sequences, ecosystems, rivers
» Internet, incoming webpage links, electrical power grids

....

We *have created power grids, for example, to supply electrical power to users over long distances, without designing any particular distribution of sizes into the system. Local grids subsequently connected with each other to form larger and larger grids of increasing complexity. The World-Wide Web was not set up simultaneously but in small pieces that later came together into a system that obeys the inverse-power law. The fact that the entire system has evolved into this particular inverse-power distribution implies that it is a stable state. The same is true for invertebrate nervous systems, which have evolved along with the organism. These non-architectural examples set the stage for what I will be talking about.*

....

FRACTAL STRUCTURE

» Pure fractals are abstract geometrical objects
» All fractals obey a universal distribution
» But there are many more non-geometrical systems that obey the universal distribution
» We may describe all stable complex systems as having "fractal properties"

KEY QUESTION IN DESIGN

» Every design contains different elements on different scales: structural, functional, etc.
» Is there any rule for determining how many elements should exist on each scale?
» YES. For adaptive design, this decision is not only intuitive, but depends upon mathematics
» NOT style-driven

DESIGN AS BRICOLAGE

» Once we have all the appropriate pieces, we can assemble them to form a whole
» Conversely, visualizing a form, we know better how to subdivide it into components
» Knowing how many pieces of each size we need solves one problem; the only question is how they all fit together!

ARCHITECTURAL SYSTEMS

» Go with a tape measure to an existing building and find its definite scales
» Say, there are several components or subdivisions of about 90cm
» Count how many there are
» Next smallest scale could be defined by components of 25cm — how many of these?

SUSTAINABILITY

» Much deeper question — is a system sustainable?
» We will examine the mathematical structure of sustainable systems
» It turns out that one common feature is how many components they have of each size — UNIVERSAL DISTRIBUTION OF SIZES

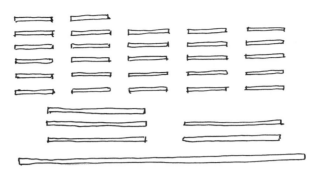

Universal distribution of sizes (showing only three scales)

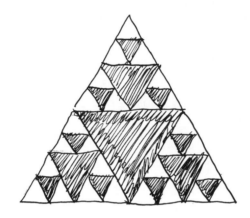

Sierpinski gasket (showing only three self-similar
scales of downward-pointing triangles)

REVISIT SIERPINSKI GASKET

» This fractal has an infinite number of smaller and smaller equilateral trian-
gles, pointing both up and down
» All the black triangles that point down are self-similar
» "HOW MANY SELF-SIMILAR TRIANGLES ARE THERE OF EACH SIZE?"
» They can be easily counted

UNIVERSAL DISTRIBUTION IN THE SIERPINSKI TRIANGLE

» Let p_i be the number of design elements of a certain size x_i
» Count how many downward-pointing black triangles there are in the Sierpinski
gasket
» Each triangle's size is $x_i = (1/2)^{i+1}$
» The number of triangles having this size equals $p_i = 3^i$

INVERSE POWER-LAW

- » The number of self-similar triangles at each size is related to their size
- » The distribution is universal, and is known as an inverse power-law
- » For the Sierpinski gasket, $p_i = 0.33/(x_i)^m$, where $m = 1.58$
- » Here, the index m is equal to the fractal dimension of the Sierpinski gasket
- » $m = D = \ln3/\ln2 = 1.58$

IN SIMPLE TERMS

- » Smaller design elements are more numerous than larger ones
- » Their relative numbers are linked to their size: **"the multiplicity of an element (design or structural) having a certain size is inversely proportional to its size"**
- » I propose that this rule applies to all adaptive design, for systemic reasons

"A UNIVERSAL RULE FOR THE DISTRIBUTION OF SIZES"

- » Derived in Chapter 3 in my book "Principles of Urban Structure", Techne Press, Amsterdam, 2005
- » Work done in collaboration with physicist Bruce J. West, who earlier worked with Jonas Salk

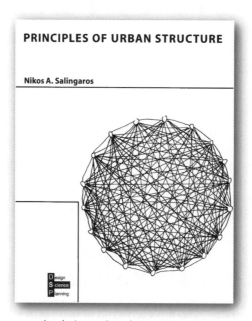

„Principles of Urban Structure"

OBVIOUS IN CITIES

» Traditional cites contain a few large buildings, many average-size buildings, very many smaller buildings, and an enormous number of structures on smaller scales: kiosks, fountains, memorials, columns, low walls, benches, bollards, etc.
» All of these cooperate to make a living city loved by human beings

NETWORKS

» Living cities also function as networks
» Connective paths obey universal distribution: a few highways, many roads, many more local streets, even more alleys, bicycle paths, and footpaths
» Modern cities skewed towards the large scale become indifferent or hostile to humans

DESTRUCTION OF PEDESTRIAN REALM

» Very simple explanation: urbanists erased geometry and network connectivity on the human range of scales — 2 m to 1 cm
» Violated universal distribution found in traditional cities (in which the hierarchy of different scales is related by some factor, and the relative abundance creates more smaller versus fewer larger objects)
» Post World-War II interventions privilege the largest scale and eliminate the small

....

Notice *that many of the smaller urban elements I mention — look at their names — are eliminated by modernist design as "clutter" that interferes with a "pure" conception of geometry and spaces. They are swept away like trash from the street. The Universal Distribution shows that this philosophy is wrong and misguided. Cities function as systems and therefore have the need for a large variety of smaller and smaller pieces far below the purely urban scale; i.e. into the human range of scales. More importantly, the network connectivity needs all of these smaller components in order to function. They are not merely "decorative" but essential pieces of a highly complex, interconnected system.*

....

3.2. FRACTAL DESIGN, ORNAMENT, AND BIOPHILIA.

NECESSARY SUBDIVISIONS

- » Which subdivisions or articulations on smaller scales make the user feel more comfortable in a space?
- » Substructure conforms to UNIVERSAL SCALING and UNIVERSAL DISTRIBUTION
- » Intermediate scales are tectonic
- » Smaller scales will be ornamental

Ornament is necessary for coherence

LACK OF ORNAMENT IS UNNATURAL!

- » Some architects will say "We want our buildings to look unnatural!"
- » We need a strong enough argument to counter this desire to shock
- » Lack of ornament violates the universal distribution, which is necessary for mathematical stability
- » No architect can counter this argument!

We perceive our environment as either having or as lacking a particular type of mathematical stability, and this has to do with whether it obeys the universal distribution of sizes. Our sensory system has evolved to perceive such qualities in the environment, and departures from the universal distribution generate alarm and hence anxiety. Traditional architecture, which obeys the universal distribution, has evolved to promote emotional wellbeing in users. Using their intuition, traditional architects the world over followed the universal distribution throughout their work, whether in creating artifacts, buildings, or cities.

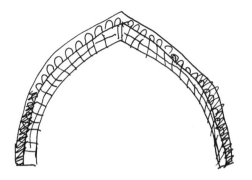

Ornament necessary for mathematical stability

Pathology is usually understood as an invasion by pathogens, or micro-organisms that cause disease, but it also includes a breakdown of the body's systems. We know that stress contributes to alter systemic balance and thus weakens the body's natural immune system, which in turn allows foreign pathogens to gain entry. Our sensory system warns us of imbalance in the working of the body's functions: e.g. pain, problems with vision, temperature, equilibrium, hormonal imbalance, etc. The same mechanism warns us whenever our environment is not fractal.

HEALTHY ENVIRONMENTS

» Adaptive architecture arises as a response to human physiology — not abstractions!
» Positive emotional response to the environment reduces stress and thus raises resistance to disease
» Emotional regeneration comes from recursive structures at every scale, and their correct combination

BIOPHILIC ORNAMENT

» First ornament was copied from plants
» First cave art represented other life forms: bears, bison, cattle
» Abstract early art uses the same mathematical structure as natural forms
» Hierarchy; fractal scaling; symmetries, rhythm

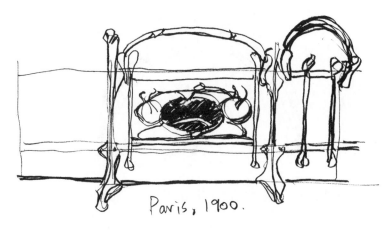

Paris, 1900.

Biophilia in Art Nouveau Architecture

Bruce West studied electrocardiograms that change immediately prior to a heart attack. A healthy heart beats in a complex manner with a beat that has a coherent fractal signal containing a universal distribution of frequencies. With the onset of pathology, the spectral characteristics of the signal shift drastically to become skewed away from the universal distribution. If this sudden shift is detected, it is a warning of an imminent heart attack. In this case, departure from the universal distribution is an indication of pathology. In the unrelated post-operative experiment, patients were housed in similar rooms, some without windows, and others with a view of an outside tree. Healing rates were faster, and the use of anti-pain medication less, in rooms with access to nature.

FRACTAL DIMENSION

» The Sierpinski gasket has dimension $D = 1.58$ (instead of 2 for a filled-in triangle)
» A fractal gasket is punched full of holes, it is perforated
» Its dimension is therefore SMALLER THAN THAT OF A PLANE, where $D = 2$ because it covers all of a 2-dimensional area
» We could use a (crinkly) fractal line to partially fill in some area, getting an accretive fractal with $D > 1$ (instead of $D = 1$ for a continuous straight line)

FRACTAL DIMENSION (CONT.)

» Recall that $D = 1$ for a continuous straight line, $D = 2$ for a filled-in plane, and $D = 3$ for a solid volume
» $D = 1.58$ for the Sierpinski gasket, which has properties between a line and a plane
» All biological, natural, and (most) architectural forms are fractals — lie in-between smooth lines, planes, and volumes!

A dimension D denotes the reach of movements in the space where something resides. For example, an ant on a wire resides in a D = 1 world, whereas the same ant on a plate resides in a D = 2 world. A moth can fly, and so it inhabits a D = 3 world. The notion of fractal dimension explores the in-between world between simple geometries such as lines, planes, and solid volumes.

WHAT THIS MEANS FOR ARCHITECTURE

- » Adaptive buildings have:
- » lines of dimension not exactly 1
- » surfaces of dimension not exactly 2
- » volumes of dimension not exactly 3
- » Architectural ornament makes sure that geometry is dimensionally "in-between"

Space is perceived according to its fractal dimension, as established by the British architect Andrew Crompton (Environment & Planning B 28, 2001, pages 243-254). I believe this to be a property of our perceptual system that applies to all animals. We seek the protection of a fractal environment that has scales corresponding to our body and its parts and avoid non-fractal open spaces. Survival originally depended upon being able to physically fit into the environment. Whenever possible, children create fractal play environments using furniture and toys: for example, cubbies, dollhouses, and secret spaces in which they and their toys fit. By adding smaller components to the existing adult space (or by subdividing it), they experience a LARGER spatial complexity. On the urban scale, historic city centers with fractal structure are experienced as LARGE, whereas in fact they are dwarfed by contemporary non-fractal urban spaces that no one wishes to use.

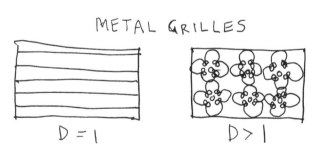

METAL GRILLES

D = 1   D > 1

Two different metal grilles: the one with in-between dimension is more interesting

FRACTAL WINDOWS

» There is a reason for using ornament in utilitarian components
» Plate-glass window shocks by juxtaposing 0-D rectangle next to 2-D wall
» Net curtains, small window panes & plants raise fractal dimension from 0 to > 1, enhance view to the outside, and also connect better to the surrounding wall, by introducing an in-between dimension

Windows with fractal structure

FRACTAL WINDOWS COME FROM ALEXANDER'S "A PATTERN LANGUAGE"

» PATTERN 238: FILTERED LIGHT
» PATTERN 239: SMALL PANES
» Two of Alexander's 253 patterns given in his monumental "A Pattern Language", Oxford University Press, New York, 1977
» Anticipated biophilic design

A Pattern Language
Towns · Buildings · Construction

Christopher Alexander

Sara Ishikawa · Murray Silverstein
WITH
Max Jacobson · Ingrid Fiksdahl-King
Shlomo Angel

„A Pattern Language"

Let's move towards some new techniques for design. In an existing building, measure the size x of components with a tape measure, as well as their multiplicity p. In a design project, use the same technique as a check of the correct distribution of sizes. Then perform the following plot, which reveals departures from the universal distribution. Such a graph also checks for the separate law of universal scaling.

MORPHOLOGICAL FEATURES

» Plot multiplicity p (how many) versus size of elements x on a log-log graph
» For a fractal distribution, we obtain evenly-spaced points on a line with negative slope $-m$, where m is the fractal dimension
» For the Sierpinski gasket, the slope of the graph equals $-D = -m = -1.58$

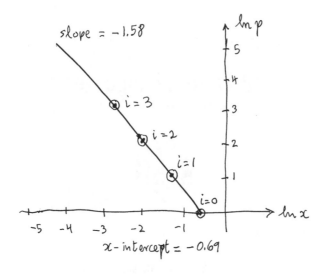

Log-log plot of p versus x

Here, the index i labels the size of each self-similar triangle in the *Sierpinski gasket: i = 0 stands for the largest triangle, i = 1 for the next smaller, and so on, with larger values for i representing smaller triangles. At the same time, the smaller triangles are more numerous, so that lnp plotted on the vertical axis, where their number is p, increases with increasing index i. The size x of the triangles decreases from the largest size, so that lnx also decreases. Because the logarithm of numbers smaller than 1 is negative, the values of lnx on the x-axis are all negative, and of course these values of lnx decrease by moving to the left.*

INTERPRET GRAPH

» Bottom point is the largest component
» Higher points represent smaller components
» Smaller components have higher multiplicity

GOOD CHECK FOR DESIGN

» Count the multiplicities of all design elements
» Plot them against their size on a log-log graph
» One criterion for coherence is for the design to show evenly-spaced points on a straight line with negative slope

TWO LAWS RELATED

> » A. Straight line in the log-log graph shows UNIVERSAL DISTRIBUTION
> » B. Evenly-spaced points on the log-log graph show UNIVERSAL SCALING
> » A design or actual structure needs to satisfy both of these related concepts
> » This graph checks for them together

At this point I could have developed a quantitative diagnostic method for the natural appearance (or not) of building façades. They would appear more natural if their intrinsic structure (as defined by their compositional elements) has the same mathematical features of a fractal such as the Sierpinski gasket, and that quality is measurable by how close they approach the above graph. I am more interested, however, in applicable design techniques rather than diagnostics. I hope that it is by now obvious that the intrinsic mathematical structure behind every architectural composition contributes to its experience by human beings. Working independently, Myriam Mahiques and Martin Laplante have analyzed building façades using a Fourier Transform, which picks up the distribution and alignment of substructures. The differences among modernist, deconstructivist, and traditional buildings is dramatic. A diagnostic tool based on Fourier Transforms remains to be developed by some enterprising student.

NECESSITY FOR LARGER ELEMENTS

> » By concentrating on the smaller subdivisions, it is easy to miss the importance of the larger ones
> » A fractal distribution necessitates a few larger elements
> » Thus, a fractal cannot be composed only from a large number of small elements

We see throughout all of history instances where an architectural tradition achieved an optimal design, with a tremendous quality of coherent ornamentation. All the complexity blends together. But then subsequent generations add more ornamentation to make the building "better", and ruin its original coherence. You cannot improve upon a perfect balance of cooperating elements. Many Rococo buildings suffer from this excessive effect, as do Romanesque churches that were ruined by later Baroque interventions. Thus, one way to ruin a perfectly balanced and coherent design is to remove the smaller scales (a minimalist revision); but another way is to fill in the necessary larger elements and thus skew the universal distribution too far towards the smaller scales.

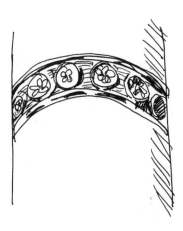

Balance ornament with plain regions

3.3. SUSTAINABLE SYSTEMS

EVOLUTION TOWARDS STABILITY

» Look at evolved systems that have all the required features to function
» Stability — those systems have worked successfully over a long time
» Evolved to overcome instabilities (otherwise they have become extinct)
» Examples found in a majority of natural and many artificial systems

EXAMPLES OF SUSTAINABLE SYSTEMS

» Ecosystems — many organisms interacting together
» Animals on top of the food chain feed on those lower down. Each level supports the entire system
» Electrical power grids (evolved)
» Internet and the world-wide web (evolved)

ANIMAL SIZE DISTRIBUTION

» In an ecosystem, count the different animals and classify them according to their mass
» We find discrete mass levels, where the heavier animals eat smaller animals (ecologists measure the mass since some animals are rounder while others are longer, so their size is not a good measure)
» Distribution is a universal distribution!
» Eliminating one level disrupts or destroys the entire ecosystem!

LESSONS FROM ECOSYSTEMS

» Stability requires redundancy
» Distinct occupants of a single niche
» Eliminating any single level (either large or small) disrupts the ecosystem (or cut a single cable in a network without redundancy)
» A gap invites invasion by alien species
» Alien species either evolve to adapt to existing ecosystem, or destroy it

---

In *stable ecological systems, the system can recover after the loss of one of its components. Some animals will evolve to become either smaller or larger so as to occupy the vacant ecological niche. It is an opportunity for them to move into a niche with less competition. In this way, island animal populations have developed a characteristic hierarchy of animals of the same type (e.g. marsupials of different mass in Australia and New Zealand). These are examples of successful adaptation from among a restricted group of original components.*

UNSUSTAINABLE SYSTEMS

» Present-day banking system (written in 2008, before the global banking collapse!)
» Large-scale industrial agriculture
» Suburban sprawl
» Skyscrapers
» Funding for urban projects and repair
» All of these emphasize the largest scale — they have no fractal properties

UNSUSTAINABLE SYSTEMS (CONT.)

» SKEWED DISTRIBUTION OF SIZES
» Christopher Alexander already pointed out that funding for urban intervention is skewed towards the largest projects
» Smaller and especially smallest projects are neglected
» Pathology of "big-scale thinking" prevents repair of living urban fabric, which requires funding satisfying a universal distribution

AGRIBUSINESS

» Tries to eliminate the local small farmer
» Depletes soil, pollutes with fertilizers
» Depends on economies of THE LARGE SCALE, sacrificing everything else
» Unsustainable in the long term
» When system nears collapse, it ends up being subsidized by big government

LAKIS POLYCARPOU

- » New York City writer
- » Q: "How can systems based on an unnatural scale distribution survive?"
- » A: "With massive financial capital, huge expenditures of energy, and sheer force of will."
- » UNSUSTAINABLE

E. F. (FRITZ) SCHUMACHER

- » Small-scale economics
- » Made a big impact on philosophers and ecologists several decades ago
- » Was only able to marginally affect mainstream economy because of the massive power of global capital
- » Still the only viable long-term solution!

"Small is Beautiful"

SCHUMACHER'S CONTRIBUTIONS

- » His work comes from economics and intuition
- » Not a mathematical analysis like ours
- » Studied systems in the developing world that worked over generations
- » Refers back to Mahatma Gandhi, who promoted small-scale economies

SOME SUSTAINABLE SOLUTIONS

» Grameen Bank in the Islamic world (begun in Bangladesh)
» Small-scale organic/local farming
» Owner-built social housing
» Focusing government onto people's problems on the local scale
» Circumvent global consumption that promotes only the largest scale

MUHAMMAD YUNUS

» Banks usually refuse to lend tiny amounts to poor persons, but will lend $100 million to one company
» MICROCREDIT — Muhammad Yunus lent very small sums out to a large number of people
» Has enormous success in boosting local economies in the developing world

SOCIAL HOUSING

» We have written a key paper on this topic (N.A.S., David Brain, Andrés Duany, Michael Mehaffy & Ernesto Philibert-Petit)
» Competition between self-build on the small scale, against government pressure to build giant large-scale housing blocs
» Builders want to make a lot of money!

SYSTEMIC STABILITY

» Narrow notion of efficiency (privileging one parameter) acts against stability
» Seeking only efficiency can eliminate diversity and hierarchical systemic support (different levels reinforcing each other)
» Artificially-supported system runs smoothly for a brief period, but eventually suffers a catastrophic collapse

Minoru Yamasaki's Pruitt-Igoe social housing high-rises in Saint Louis, Missouri were awarded an architecture prize by the American Institute of Architects. They turned into a crime-ridden wasteland. They were so dehumanizing that they were eventually dynamited by the US Government, in a rare admission of failure of its large-scale top-down applications. All over the world, Governments take money from the World Bank and use it to build giant high-rises in which to put their poor. This model is a dismal failure. Unfortunately, the ideology of geometrical efficiency that ignores collateral dehumanization leads to catastrophic social collapse.

SINGLE BUILDING

» We can consider a building as a complex system of interacting geometric parts
» Universal distribution implies certain morphological features
» Small-scale structural subdivisions distributed as in traditional architecture
» Follows from systemic stability!

CONCLUSION

» Each lecture in this series gives one building block of a larger argument
» Each argument leads to a more general awareness of structure, geometry, and human well-being in the built environment

LECTURE 4:
CELLULAR AUTOMATA
AND HYPERSPACE.

4.1. CELLULAR AUTOMATA.

4.2. SIERPINSKI CARPETS AND SEA-SHELLS.

4.3. DESIGN IN HYPERSPACE AND

CONNECTION TO THE SACRED.

4.1. CELLULAR AUTOMATA.

DESIGN AS COMPUTATION

» Unlike the previous lectures, this lecture gives no practical model for design
» Instead, I examine a union of ideas from computer science, physics, mathematics, and spirituality
» Working from analogy, I try to get into the foundations of architecture

RELATE ARCHITECTURE TO OTHER DISCIPLINES

» I relate the basis of architecture to other disciplines
» In the 20th Century, architecture has been isolated from the technological world and all of its impressive advances
» Sure, architects have applied technology, but they worked from an artistic basis. Architects today use technology, not science in the way that Christopher Alexander and I use science to understand design

SIMPLE MODELS

» Scientists confronted with a highly complex problem often create a simple model
» Capturing the essentials in a very simple model, then playing with the model helps to understand the underlying mechanism
» Work by analogy to solve the real problem, which is too complex to attack directly

CELLULAR AUTOMATA

» Arrays in which cells can assume different states
» Simplest type assume binary states: either black (on) or white (off)
» An algorithm decides how the cells change their state in discrete times
» Time: $t = 1, 2, 3, \ldots$

1-D CELLULAR AUTOMATA

» A line of cells — one dimensional model
» An algorithm generates the next state
» One such rule is: "Turn black if either neighbor is black; turn white if both neighbors are either black or white"
» For example, begin with all states white (off) except for a single black (on) in the middle

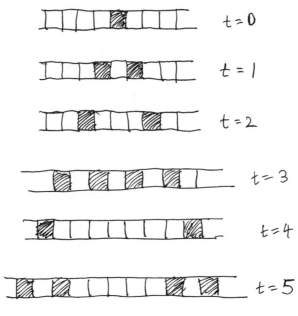

$t = 0$

$t = 1$

$t = 2$

$t = 3$

$t = 4$

$t = 5$

Rule 90 cellular automaton — picture

NOT PRESENTED AS DESIGN TOOL

» This discussion of cellular automata is directed at creating an **analogy** for understanding architectural design
» Not meant to be used directly or copied to design a building's façade!
» A simple cellular automaton does not have the right complexity to be useful in adaptive design

RULE 90 CELLULAR AUTOMATON FORMULA

» Let the state of the cell at position j and at time t be $a_j(t)$
» The value of $a_j(t)$ can either be 0 or 1
» Recursive algorithm: the cell's state at time $t + 1$ is:
» $a_j(t + 1) = \{a_{j-1}(t) + a_{j+1}(t)\}\mod2$, i.e. sum neighbor on left with neighbor on right, then take modulo two (odd numbers = 1, and even numbers = 0) to give the next state of the cell

SIMPLER FORMULATION BASED ON STATE
OF LEFT AND RIGHT NEIGHBORS

» Notation: 1 is on, 0 is off, # is either
» Simple rule for next state
» 1#1 and 0#0 both become #0#
» 0#1 and 1#0 both become #1#

INITIAL CONDITION

» Next state of a cellular automaton depends upon the previous state
» Initial conditions determine all later development
» This example began with just one black pixel (on), and the pattern grows to infinite length

DIFFERENT CELLULAR AUTOMATA

» We used rule 90 in Wolfram's classification: Stephen Wolfram, "A New Kind of Science", Wolfram Media, Champaign, Illinois, USA, 2002.
» A different rule will define a distinct cellular automaton

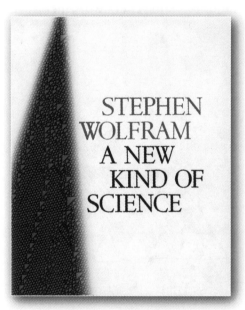

„A New Kind of Science"

NEAREST NEIGHBOR

» Many different types of cellular automata
» Rule 90 is a "nearest-neighbor" rule
» Simplest interaction of "on" elements — only with their nearest neighbors
» Shortest possible interaction distance
» LONG-RANGE PATTERN RESULTS FROM THIS (LOCAL) RULE

MISGUIDED APPLICATIONS

» Some architects are beginning to apply Wolfram's results directly to design
» I believe they are mistaken

»   Creating non-adaptive forms that look pretty, but are unsuitable for buildings
»   Wolfram's cellular automata are just a set of examples useful for analogies, not for design models

4.2. SIERPINSKI CARPETS AND SEA-SHELLS

COSMATI TILES?

»   Cellular automaton Rule 90 generates a digitized version of the Sierpinski fractal triangle (with the above initial condition beginning with only one cell on)
»   Different initial conditions will generate distinct fractal triangles (one is constructed later)

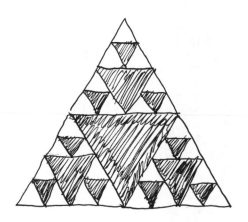

Sierpinski fractal triangle

ALGORITHMIC DESIGN RULES

»   I am laying down the logical framework for adaptive algorithms
»   Design rules should not produce a mathematical fractal, but will generate a complex structure — a building or a city — with many of the coherent features of a fractal

We are learning from a very simple but unrealistic mathematical model. An example shows how generating complexity from local (nearest-neighbor) rules can create an ordered large-scale structure. Buildings and cities will not look like these diagrams, because their complexity is on a different level altogether. These exercises prepare us to understand the real-life problems of architectural design.

WEAVING A CARPET

»   Human activity over Asia, the Middle East, and the entire Islamic world for millennia
»   Knot one horizontal line of the carpet at a time — similar to 1-D cellular automaton
»   Some cultures sing the 1-D pattern that gives each line, as it is being woven
»   The result is a two-dimensional fabric

SPACE-TIME DIAGRAM

»   A 1-D cellular automaton evolves in time by changing its state/appearance
»   Show the time dimension of its evolution by displaying its states at different times next to each other. This results in a 2-D space-time diagram (with x-t axes)
»   The diagram is a two-dimensional carpet: the space axis goes x across horizontally, the cellular automaton, and the time axis t goes down vertically (note that carpet weavers add new rows on top, however, not below)

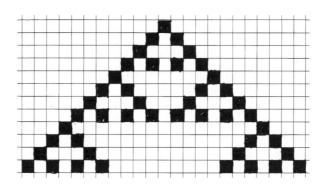

Sierpinski carpet

SIERPINSKI CARPET (CONT.)

»   Subsequent states of 1-D cellular automaton Rule 90 "weave" the 2-D Sierpinski triangle
»   Carpet is a DIGITIZED fractal, because there is a minimum pixel size — one cell
»   As it adds more rows of cells, or "lines of knots", the Sierpinski carpet gets closer to a mathematical fractal
»   A perforated fractal has been created by an algorithm

EMERGENCE OF PATTERNS

»   Visual example shows "emergence"
»   A recursive 1-D algorithm (on a line) involving only nearest-neighbor interactions generates a nested design — a 2-D fractal (on a plane)
»   Nothing in this cellular automaton leads us to expect such complex long-range patterns that can be seen only in 2-D

ARCHITECTURAL CONCLUSIONS, BY ANALOGY

» Simplest possible 1-D binary algorithm generates large-scale order
» All characteristics of coherence are present — scaling hierarchy, scaling symmetry, scaling distribution, subsymmetries, etc.
» Can we use simple rules to create great buildings and cities?
» YES! Form languages, Smart Code, etc.

JUST PROVED AN IMPORTANT POINT

» New Urbanist codes, like the Smart Code of Andrés Duany and Elizabeth Plater-Zyberk work because they generate adaptive environments (and consequently real estate prices go up)
» I just showed by analogy that **using the correct algorithms, it is possible to generate complex environments**

EMERGENCE IN GENERAL

» A very simple rule generates a complex pattern not explicit in the initial code
» Self-similarity, scaling coherence, and scaling distribution all arise from an algorithm acting on the smallest scale
» Emergent geometrical patterns are seen only in a higher dimension than the one the algorithm acts upon

FIRST ANIMAL TO APPLY A CELLULAR AUTOMATON TO BUILD

» Marine mollusks generate a fractal pattern on their shells: *Tent Olive Shell* (South America), *Damon's Volute* (Western Australia), *Textile Cone* (Indo-Pacific), *Glory of the Seas* (Pacific)
» Animal lays down 1-D pattern one row at a time, as it grows the lip of its shell
» Patterns are very roughly Sierpinski-like (but only surface decoration!)

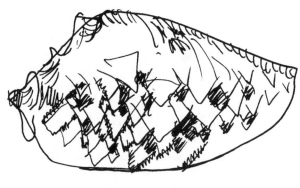

Seashell

AMAZING

» The mollusk is growing its house using a fractal pattern — algorithmic design!
» The mollusk never gets to see the outside of its shell; it never goes out, and its eyes are not as highly developed
» While the mollusk is alive, the shell pattern is covered by an organic membrane

THE SIERPINSKI TRIANGLE AND THE BINOMIAL THEOREM

» Binomial coefficients are numbers in the expansion of $a + b$ to the n-th power
» All the binomial coefficients can be computed from Pascal's triangle
» Re-compute Pascal's triangle modulo 2 (odd = 1, even = 0)
» Becomes the digitized Sierpinski triangle

$$(a+b)^2 = a^2 + 2ab + b^2$$

$$(a+b)^3 = a^3 + 3a^2b + 3ab^2 + b^3$$

$$(a+b)^4 =$$

$$a^4 + 4a^3b + 6a^2b^2 + 4ab^3 + b^4$$

Binomial expansions

```
              1
           1     1
         1    2    1
       1    3    3    1
     1    4    6    4    1
   1    5   10   10    5    1
  1   6   15   20   15   6    1
 1   7   21   35   35   21   7    1
```

Pascal's triangle of coefficients in the binomial expansions

SIMPLE ALGORITHM FOR GENERATING THE ROWS OF PASCAL'S TRIANGLE

» Begin with the zeroth power — everything equals 1
» The first power has coefficients 1, 1
» Add the two numbers to get 1, 1 + 1 = 2, 1
» Next line has 1, 1 + 2 = 3, 2 + 1 = 3, 1
» Continue to generate more rows…

Every number in Pascal's triangle is the sum of the immediate entries just above that number. For example, 21 = 6 + 15, and 35 = 15 + 20, etc. Therefore, the binomial coefficients can be generated just by simple addition of numbers, without having to expand the expression (a + b) to some power. But this procedure is just a mysterious rule that does not show the origin of these numbers.

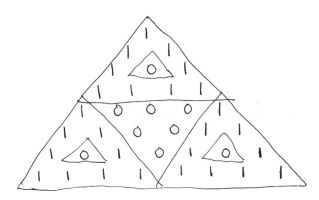

Pascal's triangle modulo 2 (odd = 1, even = 0) becomes Sierpinski

CLASSIFICATION OF CELLULAR AUTOMATA

» Wolfram has classified all 256 possible 1-D cellular automata with binary states (on-off) and nearest-neighbor interactions
» Twenty of them (8%) generate variants of the Sierpinski gasket, others are not regular
» Generative codes are very few among all possible architectural algorithms

SELECTION OF ALGORITHMS

» Even among the simplest cellular automata (nearest-neighbor, two-state systems) the majority does not generate any coherent designs!
» There are infinitely more (long-range, multi-state, etc.) cellular automata
» Rule 90 is useful because it is seen in biological structures, and is also related to the Binomial Theorem

A DIFFERENT INITIAL CONDITION

» Use Rule 90 with different initial condition
» The same cellular automaton can generate many distinct nested hierarchical patterns
» Development depends upon the initial state
» For example, begin with three black pixels (on) distributed as (11001)

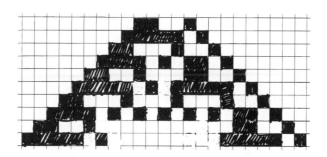

Rule 90, different initial condition

ANALOGOUS IMPLICATIONS FOR DESIGN

» Adaptive design is highly dependent upon initial conditions: existing structures, surroundings, human needs, etc.
» The same design algorithm will result in drastically distinct end-products
» **The proper algorithm can be used to design buildings and cities that are each distinct because they adapt to local conditions**

With one stroke, we have hopefully laid to rest the common terror that traditional form languages restrict architectural creativity. This statement is mathematically false. We can use an adaptive design algorithm with a traditional form language to design different buildings depending upon different initial conditions. Classical and traditional architects know that. By adapting to local conditions, buildings and cities become unique while using the same algorithm. And there exist many distinct adaptive design algorithms that have evolved over the millennia of human existence. Using these algorithms with different local conditions makes possible an infinity of innovative results.

FORMAL DESIGN IS NOT ADAPTIVE

» Can be of either two forms:
» A. NON-ALGORITHMIC, WHICH ONLY IMPOSES PRECONCEIVED FORMS
» B. ALGORITHMIC BUT NON-ADAPTIVE, NOT RESPONSIVE TO INITIAL CONDITIONS
» Formal designs are self-referential — they could all look the same

ALGORITHMS IN NATURE

» Nature only uses sustainable algorithms
» Non-sustainable algorithms die out!
» Darwinian selection based on survival
» This is SELECTION OF ALGORITHMS instead of SELECTION OF FORMS that we normally think of as the result of evolution

4.3. DESIGN IN HYPERSPACE
AND CONNECTION TO THE SACRED

INDISPUTABLE EFFECT

» An entirely speculative direction
» Nevertheless, topic is fundamentally important to architecture
» For millennia, human beings have sought to connect to the sacred realm through architecture

METAPHYSICAL QUESTIONS

» Christopher Alexander talks about connecting to a larger coherence
» We experience this connection — a visceral feeling — in a great religious building or place of great natural beauty
» Hassan Fathy talked about the sacred structure in everyday environments

Islamic Architecture

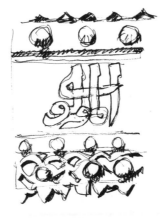

Cairo, 1480

Islamic architectural details

CONNECTING VIA ARCHITECTURE

» Talking about connecting viscerally to a building makes people profoundly uneasy
» For millennia, our ancestors built sacred places and buildings that connect us to something beyond everyday reality
» Today's western culture does not accept this as possible

By dismissing the most important part of architecture — the profound connection to places and buildings — we have lost part of our sense of being. This reveals the total wrong-headedness of architecture in our times, especially in Western culture. Islamic architecture searched for this connection, and succeeded in many cases. I will try to talk about this connection in mathematical terms by looking at processes occurring in spaces of different dimensions. Begin by reviewing the three spatial dimensions, then use the experimental basis of physics to discuss higher dimensions, i.e. this speculative discussion is not based on mathematical abstractions, but on the structure of matter.

EXCURSIONS TO HIGHER DIMENSIONS

» Line — one dimension (1-D)
» Plane — two dimensions (2-D)
» Volume — three dimensions (3-D)
» In mathematics, it is perfectly normal to work in any number of dimensions
» From physics, we know that ordinary matter exists in several dimensions

PHYSICAL DIMENSIONS

» Three spatial dimensions: x, y, z that our senses perceive directly
» Next dimensions distinguish elementary particles (but are not perceived directly)
» Spin: distinguishes Bosons from Fermions
» Isospin: distinguishes Nucleons
» Hypercharge: distinguishes shorter-lived elementary particles

ARCHITECTURE IN HYPERSPACE

» Imagine a complex design or structure defined in more than 3-D
» This structure is richly patterned
» We cannot fully perceive its symmetries because of our perceptual limitations
» The only features we can see are sections of the whole n-D structure

CENTRAL CONJECTURE

» WE CONNECT TO A HIGHER REALM ONLY THROUGH COHERENT COMPLEX STRUCTURES
» Coherence and symmetries of form make possible the continuation into symmetries in other dimensions
» Most 20th-Century and contemporary buildings restrict forms to 3-D or less because they are minimalist or disordered (lacking coherent complexity)

ANALOGY: DESIGN SECTIONS

» We used a 1-D cellular automaton to construct the 2-D Sierpinski carpet
» By analogy, people build 3-D material structures that could generate a larger coherent structure within n-D hyperspace
» We could thus connect to the larger n-D entity, which is more than what we can see

PATTERNS IN n-D

» With the Sierpinski gasket, it is not possible to deduce its symmetric large-scale nested patterns from any single section (i.e. from a single line)
» Nevertheless, we do observe regularity in each cellular automaton with Rule 90
» Geometrical coherence in what we see implies a larger coherence in n-D

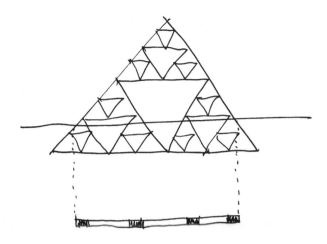

Section through Sierpinski gasket does not reveal its full coherent complexity, but only hints at its existence

IMAGINED STRUCTURE

» Sierpinski: patterns shown in any 1-D section imply that the original has complex, coherent structure in 2-D
» Self-similarity and scaling of the complex 2-D object show only as reduced coherent patterns on the 1-D cellular automaton

HOW CAN WE CONNECT TO COHERENT STRUCTURES IN n-D ?

» Actually, this deeper question is easily answered with mathematics
» If we inhabit a space that is bounded, then we cannot connect to something outside it
» By going to one more dimension, we can jump over the boundary and connect
» Example: it is possible to jump in 3-D space to get over 2-D boundary

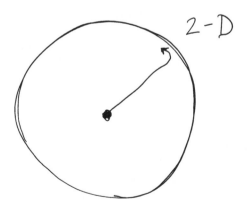

If we are bounded in 2-D ...

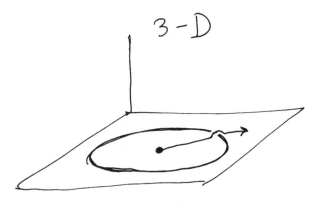

... we could jump in 3-D to get over the boundary

PHILOSOPHICAL/RELIGIOUS QUESTIONS

» We have raised questions — without answering them — about connecting to a higher state of order
» How can we make a "jump" out of the physical 3-D space of buildings so as to connect to a realm beyond 3-D?
» Religions tell us that it is indeed possible

PHYSICAL/MATHEMATICAL QUESTIONS

» Are the additional dimensions of our existence INTERIOR or EXTERIOR?
» Spiritual approach tends to imagine a world "outside" our everyday realm
» But physics has discovered dimensions "inside" — the internal symmetries of elementary particles

CONNECTING

» Conjectural picture presented here highlights questions about connecting to a higher order
» Alexander addresses this topic, using empirical evidence presented in "The Nature of Order, Book 4: The Luminous Ground"

LIMITS OF BIOLOGY?

» How high can we rise in our emotional connection and still explain it biologically?
» Emotional highs come from love, music, art, architecture, poetry, literature
» Mechanisms of response are all biological (sensory apparatus), although the most important elements are still incompletely understood

CONDITIONS FOR SACRED CONNECTION

» I'm interested in geometrical, not mystical properties
» Connection is achieved through dance, music, art, and architecture
» Patterns, regularity, repetition, nesting, hierarchy, scaling, fractal structure — common feature of all

SPIRITUALITY

» Highest artistic expression is related to religion
» Bach, Mozart, Botticelli, Michelangelo; anonymous artists and architects of Islamic art and architecture, mystics of the world
» By seeking God, human beings attain highest level of connection to universe

QUESTIONS THAT TOUCH ON RELIGION

» Without specifying any particular organized religion, spirituality can lead to connectivity
» Same mechanism as biophilia? Maybe — only more advanced and more intense — source of emotional nourishment
» Can we transcend biological connection to achieve an even higher spiritual connection?

MANIFESTATION OF THE SACRED

» Religious belief itself is abstract, resident in the mind
» But connection occurs through geometry, senses, music, rhythm, color
» Religious connection is very physical, oftentimes intensely so
» This physical connection gives us the materialization of sacred experience

DANCE — TEMPORAL RHYTHM

» Bharatnatyam, classical Indian dancing
» African shamanic dance & Native American religious dance
» Whirling dervishes in Mevlana, Turkey & Hassidic dances
» Mystical dance forms contain geometric qualities of scaling coherence

MUSIC — RHYTHM

» In the Classical West: Masses of Bach, Haydn, and Mozart
» Show fractal temporal structure — inverse power-law scaling
» Sacred chant in all religions connects
» Holy days: Byzantine Easter service, Passion Plays, Kol Nidre during Yom Kippur, Buddhist ceremonial chant

SACRED ARCHITECTURE

» All over the world, the House of God displays the qualities we seek to the highest possible extent
» Independent of particular religion or style
» Found among all religious building types
» Architects of the past instinctively built according to rules for scaling coherence

CONCLUSION

» All the examples I have mentioned have common mathematical qualities
» Fractals, symmetries, rhythm, hierarchy, scaling distribution, etc.
» Deliberate creations by humanity the world over trying to connect to something out there — or is it inside?

LECTURE 5:
DESIGN AS COMPUTATION
WITH CONSTRAINTS.

5.1. ARCHITECTURAL HARMONY

COMPUTE THE ARCHITECTURAL HARMONY

» GOAL OF COMPUTATION: improve coherence of the design by successive steps
» Mathematical model of "harmony" given in my book "A Theory of Architecture"
» Harmony estimates density of symmetries, connections, scaling coherence, universal scaling, universal distribution, etc.

San Miniato al Monte, Florence

ESTIMATE THE HARMONY

» Reflectional symmetries on all scales = 2/2
» Translational and rotational symmetries on all scales = 2/2
» Scaling symmetries = 1/2
» Geometrical connections = 2/2
» Color harmonization = 1/2
» Sum to get total harmony = 8/10 = 80%

METHOD OF ESTIMATION

» Simplest estimate for each property seen in obvious design characteristics:
» NONE = 0
» SOME, NOTICEABLE = 1
» A GREAT DEAL = 2
» Each of the 5 components of the architectural harmony adds up to give a percentage measure

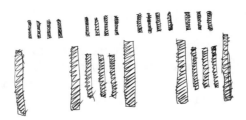

Translational symmetries in the façade

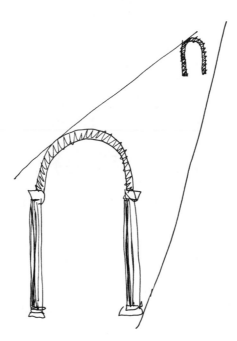

Scaling symmetries in the façade

In trying to establish an honest architectural pedagogy, I introduced simple measures such as the "architectural harmony". My intent is to provide architecture students with a set of simple numerical estimates, which can then be used to analyze architectural form; compare different buildings; judge the coherence and qualities of one's design so that it can evolve towards human adaptivity, etc. Not surprisingly, nothing like this exists in architectural education today: there are no quantitative measures of design parameters, and therefore the process of judging a design is entirely subjective. This situation is easily manipulated to impose non-adaptive fashionable styles.

5.2. CHRISTOPHER ALEXANDER'S
THEORY OF CENTERS

A "CENTER" AS A FOCUS

» Basic notion describing the ordering process in nature (and in architecture)
» The geometry of mutually reinforcing focal points
» Independent from patterns already obtained via interaction between geometry and social structure

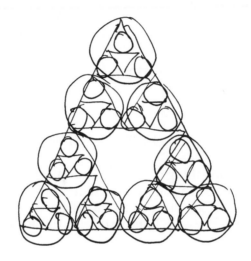

Recursive points of focus (circles within larger circles) in the Sierpinski gasket

FOCUS AND CONDENSATION IN FRACTALS

» Self-similarity and the universal distribution require that the details in fractals are not uniformly distributed
» Smaller scales focus in particular regions of a fractal where subdivision occurs

THE THEORY OF CENTERS

» A "center" is a visual field that is the focus of a region
» The region that focuses on a "center" can be of any size
» Centers help to tie the space together by reinforcement
» Recursion leads to fractal properties

CENTERS — STRUCTURE-VOID DUALITY

» Two types of centers: "defined" and "implied" (my own terminology)
» Either a well-defined structure in the middle is surrounded by a looser boundary; or a void is surrounded by a structured boundary
» Mathematically, these two types are dual to each other

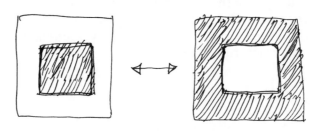

Figure-ground duality

A. "DEFINED" OR "EXPLICIT" CENTERS

» A region in which something right in the middle focuses the structure
» The focal point draws attention to the actual center of a region
» Examples: fountain or sculpture in the middle of plaza; window or door centered in the middle of a wall; light fixture in the center of a ceiling; medallion in paving

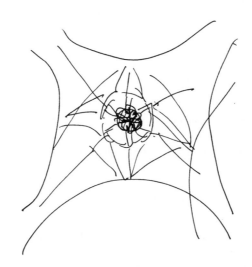

Medallion is focal point of ceiling design

Window is focal point of plain wall

B. "IMPLIED" OR "LATENT" CENTERS

» A region that focuses on its central point, but where the middle is empty
» Surrounding structure is helping to focus attention towards the interior
» This is a boundary effect — the boundary is focusing on the implied center
» Examples: courtyard enclosed by decorated walls; cloister; decorated arch

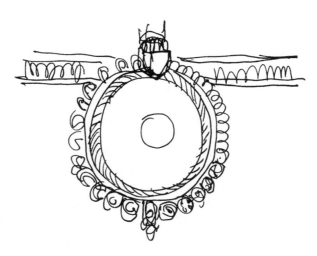

Highly ornamented window frame focuses on center

Monumental arch focuses on passageway

GEOMETRICAL FOCUS

» Both "defined" and "implied" centers are the foci for their surrounding structures
» "Defined" and "implied" centers can overlap, thus helping each other
» In a coherent design, all the centers cooperate to reinforce each other
» Smaller centers combine to form larger centers — recursive property

ALGORITHM FOR GENERATING CENTERS

» Create both strong "defined" and "implicit" centers on a particular scale
» Place/create smaller centers so that they are nested within larger centers
» Use symmetries to make centers cooperate so they support each other geometrically
» Success means that centers blend together

While performing the design computations, both defined and implicit centers created on different scales and positions begin to blend together to define a complex coherent whole. In this process, one center becomes a subcenter of another larger center as centers begin to blend into each other, and it becomes impossible to distinguish overlapping centers, to identify individual centers, or to say anything about the actual size of any individual center. We have a complex structure with internal regions of focus. The coherence of the whole is due to the emergent properties generated by cooperating centers.

ADAPTIVITY AND ASYMMETRY

» We are encouraging the formation of a high density of local symmetries, not an overall symmetry
» ASYMMETRY arises from adaptation, usually seen on larger scales
» But there needs to be a reason for asymmetry, not just personal whim

ALEXANDER'S FIRST ALGORITHM

» "Every time you create a center on a particular scale, make sure that it reinforces the centers on the immediately smaller scale, and the centers on the immediately larger scale"
» From Alexander's "The Nature of Order", Book 1

ALEXANDER'S SECOND ALGORITHM

» "Begin by visualizing the whole. Then identify the scale that is the weakest, or is missing. Create or intensify a center on that scale. The new center must reinforce all existing centers on its own scale, as well as follow rule 1."
» From Alexander's "The Nature of Order", Book 3

EXAMPLE: FIND A WEAKNESS

» Problem: some part of your design feels wrong
» Don't just adjust that piece, but look at that SCALE of the problematic piece in the entire design
» Ask: WHAT IS THE BEST CENTER THAT REINFORCES THIS SCALE?
» Solution: implement that center, rather than adjusting the original faulty piece. This idea re-orients design from thinking about individual pieces, to thinking about particular scales

STARTING FROM WEAKNESS

» Usually start from the site, which may contain a weak system of centers
» Apply successful transformations
» Each step creates new centers, or reinforces existing weak centers
» All centers reinforce each other to create a coherent whole

THE FIRST SET OF LEITNER DIAGRAMS

» Helmut Leitner uses simple visuals to grasp the center-generating transformations
» 1. Stepwise
» 2. Reversible
» 3. Structure-preserving
» 4. Design from weakness
» 5. New from existing

1. STEPWISE:
PERFORM ONE STEP AT A TIME

Already, we run into a problem with the architectural education of recent decades, where students are taught to envision a project as if completed "all at once". This is, after all, what famous contemporary architects are supposed to do, following the myth of divine inspiration. It thus becomes very difficult to convince a young architect to design one step at a time.

2. REVERSIBLE:
TEST DESIGN DECISIONS USING MODELS; "TRIAL AND ERROR"; IF IT DOESN'T WORK, UNDO IT

Another deep problem, which reveals the inadequacy of present-day design training: how does a practitioner judge whether a design "works" or not? Otherwise, an architect has no means of judging if an individual step has indeed led closer to an adaptive solution. The only means of doing so is to use criteria of coherence and adaptivity, not abstract or formal design.

3. STRUCTURE-PRESERVING:
EACH STEP BUILDS UPON WHAT IS ALREADY THERE

4. DESIGN FROM WEAKNESS:
EACH STEP IMPROVES COHERENCE

Again, part of the same fundamental problem we already encountered: how to identify the precise location where an evolving design happens to be "weak". This can only be done on the basis of adaptivity and coherence, otherwise one risks privileging a non-adaptive component that looks "exciting" instead of revising it to create an improved coherence.

5. NEW FROM EXISTING:
EMERGENT STRUCTURE COMBINES WHAT IS
ALREADY THERE INTO NEW FORM

If you create a large building all at once, guided by the customary "great flash of genius", and it is wrong, it is wrong in thousands of different ways. By contrast, Alexander suggests a stepwise method of design, which makes corrections possible by providing a methodology and checks that catch mistakes before they develop into monsters. Even a very modest building is the product of a very large number of design decisions. It is mathematically impossible to make all those decisions simultaneously. The "soul" of a building, be it a modest or great building, is due to emergent properties, which cannot possibly be conceived at the beginning of the design process.

FUTURE SOFTWARE

- » With time, we can program these algorithmic rules
- » Pattern recognition is a problem of major interest in computer intelligence and vision
- » Model for estimating the coherence or "life" of structures is developed in "A Theory of Architecture", following Alexander's "15 Fundamental Properties"

Architects *today have expectations of using computers for design beyond their current application as graphic design tools. This is a realizable goal, but any success towards achieving adaptive computer design depends totally upon the rules programmed into the software system. At the present time, design software has a very strong but hidden basis of Bauhaus design rules, and that is why when trying to generate a graphic with human qualities, one has to fight against the software's own preferences. It is doubtlessly only a matter of time before we have more adaptive design software available, but the software companies have to respond to client demand if they are going to invest in bringing such software to market.*

INCOMPLETENESS THEOREM

- » Software will never substitute for a human designer
- » "Living structure" is not possible just from a mathematical algorithm
- » Not enough cognitive capacity!
- » Computer algorithm is interesting and will be very useful for saving effort

UNIVERSAL DISTRIBUTION MERGES TO BECOME A FIELD EFFECT

- » Centers obey universal distribution: few large ones, some of intermediate size, many smaller ones
- » Achieving harmony, however, blurs the identity of each center
- » Coherence is a "field effect" — the secret of our greatest architecture, as described by Alexander in "The Nature of Order"

5.3. DESIGN AS COMPUTATION

SEQUENCE OF STEPS

» Christopher Alexander views successive steps of adaptive design as steps in a complex computation
» Take initial condition as defined by the site, and by successive steps transform it into the final coherent design
» Computation of finite number of steps

ALGORITHMS ARE RECURSIVE

» Algorithm is repeated until a desired level of harmony in achieved, or until the resources run out
» With each succeeding step, coherence of total design is improved
» Next step locates (makes obvious) new bottleneck to coherence

You *strive to improve the coherence of the design until it is "good enough", which in this context means adaptive to human uses and sensibilities. Then you can stop and declare the computation finished. This is not a computation directed towards a unique result, but rather a successive computation that should lead towards any one of several satisfactory results having a high degree of coherence. Remember Herbert Simon's concept of "satisficing" in a complex process: a non-optimal solution that satisfies a set of criteria. As long as the coherence of the whole is increasing with each step of the computation, we are moving in the right direction. Deciding when to stop is up to the designer.*

WHAT IS OUR ALGORITHM?

» Alexander's first and second algorithms (given above)
» A. Identify the weakest or missing center that forms a bottleneck in the harmony of the configuration
» B. Intensify that center
» C. Act both locally and globally

... BUT THERE ARE MORE

» These are just two of several algorithms acting together
» More process principles are needed for computation
» Process concepts are not yet as well developed as structural concepts
» Refer to Leitner's first set of diagrams

WHAT ARE THE CONSTRAINTS?

- » 1. Brief of project (a) — functions
- » 2. Brief of project (b) — human needs
- » 3. Biophilic considerations — human feelings of wellbeing
- » 4. Patterns from a Pattern Language
- » 5. Connecting to the surroundings

PATTERNS AS COMPLEX SOCIO-GEOMETRIC "CENTERS"

- » Socio-geometrical ways of behavior
- » Repeated rediscovery of useful configurations in buildings and cities
- » Classified in Alexander's book: "A Pattern Language"
- » Come from participatory design
- » Not a pure geometrical concept

When "A Pattern Language" was first published in 1977, architects immediately assumed that it was a design manual, and used it to generate some very interesting buildings. Those buildings, despite their positive human qualities, lack an overall coherence, and people did not understand why this was happening. The reason is that the Patterns provide essential and necessary constraints, and not a design method in itself. The actual design algorithm was developed by Alexander, but only many years later.

WHAT ARE THE PROGRAMMING TOOLS?

- » 1. Alexander's 15 fundamental properties: provide the "code" in which the algorithm is written and implemented (next lecture)
- » 2. Process principles: to be developed more
- » 3. Connecting concepts: universal scaling, universal distribution, wide boundaries, architectural harmony, centers, etc.

GOAL OF COMPUTATION

- » Goal is not what one would expect!
- » Algorithm does not compute the typology of the building (e.g. house)
- » **Algorithm computes harmony, and each step proceeds by improving the harmony**
- » Function of building lies in the constraints!

FORMAL DECOMPOSITION

» Algorithm broken up into specific computational loops (in theory)
» But this decomposition does not even touch the implementation problems!
» How do we achieve "living structure"?
» Not only geometrical harmony
» Need to incorporate patterns

HIGH-LEVEL DESCRIPTION

» Algorithm: larger main loop computes architectural harmony
» Several nested secondary iterative loops act as constraints:
» — project brief; patterns from "A Pattern Language"; universal scaling; universal distribution…

Architectural typology arises from the constraints, not from a directed algorithm. One computes ever-increasing harmony, and it is the constraints that push the design towards the client brief, e.g. "house" instead of "restaurant" or "church". One should not expect this type of adaptive algorithm to directly compute a "house", even though a client is paying for this end result! A Darwinian selection acts to choose among the different possibilities, to give a building that exquisitely fits the needs of the client. It is also true that an adapted building can be subsequently re-used for a different need by a successive user: a great palace becomes a set of offices; a set of offices becomes an art museum, etc. We feel at ease in those adapted buildings, independently of their present use.

NON-ADAPTIVE ARCHITECTURAL DESIGN

» A drawing based on images has nothing to do with an adaptive building
» An adaptive design must be computed!
» Human mind is the best pattern computer
» The number of computations is proportional to the complexity of the desired result
» There can be no shortcuts to final form

MOST DESIGN IS MEMORY-BASED

» No computation at all
» Retrieval from a memory bank
» Even if architect is convinced he/she is being totally innovative, design is usually coming out of subconscious memory
» Harmony-seeking computations are rarely applied by architects in the industrial world

GOOD AND BAD MEMORY

» Stored proven patterns are good; exist in distinct cultures
» Evolved over generations, tested and survived by adaptive selection
» But recycling of faulty design patterns gives bad designs
» Therefore: need periodic checks for the correctness of stored patterns

ALGORITHMIC CHECKS

» Coherence and cooperation of different elements among different levels of scale
» Analogous to the coherence of a fractal
» Alexander's fifteen fundamental properties help achieve living quality
» Global-local geometrical property

The process of design needs to be contrasted with, and distinguished from simply finding a solution. Locating a unique solution involves exploratory steps towards a fixed but hidden result. A sequence of steps (which is not unique) leads one closer to discovering the solution (which is lying there only waiting to be revealed). Design instead requires one to closely follow carefully-defined steps (with very little randomness) towards an initially undetermined (and not unique) end-product. In the process of design the exploratory method is fundamentally different from finding a solution, because in design, the steps themselves influence and create the final state. What are known as "Design Methods" constitute an established discipline that discusses the design process using flowcharts and bubble diagrams. Following the arrows and loops between rectangles, circles, and ellipses in these diagrams is supposed to describe a general algorithmic procedure for the creative process, which can teach you how to design. Unfortunately, I have never found such methods useful in the least, and, in my mind, the basic problem of design has to be understood in an entirely different manner.

EMERGENCE

» A very simple algorithm acting on the smallest scale generates a complex pattern with long-range geometrical features
» Complex geometrical properties emerge from recursion
» They are not obvious in the initial code

ALEXANDER'S HARMONY-SEEKING PROCESS
IS MORE THAN EMERGENT!

» Emergence is only a two-way process
» Smaller components cooperate to create a larger whole — link small with large
» Harmony-seeking computations have an additional element — three-way process
» Whole interacts with an even larger external entity — small, with large, with outside

A building interacts with its exterior region, whether this is planned or not. The more intelligently a building has been adapted to its surroundings, the better quality urban fabric is formed immediately around it. We cannot control the region outside our building, but it does influence the design. A consequence of adapting a building to the outside is a possible asymmetry in the building itself. Emergent features of our building are influenced by its internal components as they build up to a larger whole (which is the building). By adapting to the surroundings, the final adaptive result will encompass a far broader region than the confines of the lot we are given to work with.

5.4. COMPUTATIONAL REDUCIBILITY

HOW MUCH COMPUTATION?

» General misunderstanding of how much work is required to create a complex system
» Design generates complex systems
» Everyone wants shortcuts
» Some shortcuts compromise system coherence and functionality

Let us assume that the reader has understood the necessity for step-by-step computation of an adaptive design. The resulting design emerges as a complex interactive system. In order to abandon the all-at-once (but non-adaptive) design method in current use, a practitioner would like to know how much time and effort he/she has to invest in the new, stepwise algorithmic design method. For this reason, it is essential to discuss the number of steps that are required to build up a complex system in general. Even though this discussion is of central concern to design, it must be framed in terms of computation and complex systems.

COMPUTATIONAL PROCESSES

» All processes can be viewed as computations (Stephen Wolfram)
» Both human and natural processes
» Form develops by changing its state on various different levels
» Life continuously changes materials of organism, but maintains form template

COMPUTATIONAL REDUCIBILITY

» Adaptive systems evolve, with each step being a computation
» In simple physical systems, we don't need to duplicate the amount of computational effort, but can shortcut to final state — i.e., use a formula
» Simple case is COMPUTATIONALLY REDUCIBLE

COMPUTATIONAL IRREDUCIBILITY

» In irreducibly complex systems, there are no formulas for finding the final state
» Computation of final state requires the same effort as the system has gone through to create itself — no reduction
» Stephen Wolfram's "computational irreducibility"

THE REDUCIBILITY FALLACY

» Design that is adaptive needs to compute a large number of steps
» The algorithm is usually recursive
» Such a process is COMPUTATIONALLY IRREDUCIBLE
» **It is therefore impossible to make a top-down design so that it is adaptive**

··

A reducible design process would be extremely fast (and hence economically desirable) because one could find a shortcut to the final result. An adaptive design process is computationally irreducible, however, and we are fooling ourselves if we think that we can impose a template, or somehow reach a final state through a formula or shortcut. Top-down design can never be adaptive. Adaptive design is necessarily the end-result of a recursive computation with feedback. The best of traditional design methods combine top-down methods with bottom-up methods.

··

GENERAL PROCEDURE

» Decompose design problem into more tractable subunits or components
» Decomposition is dictated by experience
» Employ known methods (relying upon precedent) to evaluate subroutines
» Re-assemble partial results into final result
» Initial decomposition determines re-assembly

GENERAL PROCEDURE (CONT.)

» Require selection criteria to be able to eliminate false positives
» How do you recognize false steps?

» Again, this relies upon precedent (constraints such as Patterns; traditional form languages such as Classical and others)
» Process is successful if large scale structure is adaptive, not if it is strange or irrelevant

----

Here we are going into the details of computational processes that explore a solution space in order to locate one or more acceptable adaptive solutions. These topics are not usually studied in architecture, but lie in the domain of mathematics and computer science. The enormous complexity of architectural and urban design problems requires algorithmic decomposition and implementation of search methods. In these lectures, I have tried to outline methods for dealing with this complexity. The alternative, which is followed by architects working in recent decades, is to ignore the complexity of the problem and to impose a non-adaptive simplistic solution, oftentimes with added but irrelevant complexity that has nothing to do with satisfying user needs.

CONCLUSION: COMPUTATIONAL EQUIVALENCE

» Classical and traditional architects follow part of our algorithm for design
» From computational irreducibility, all adaptive design algorithms are computationally equivalent
» Any computationally inequivalent design algorithm cannot be adaptive

LECTURE 6:
UNIVERSAL MORPHOLOGICAL RULES.

6.1. ALEXANDER'S 15 FUNDAMENTAL PROPERTIES

6.2. THREE LAWS OF ARCHITECTURE

6.1. ALEXANDER'S FIFTEEN
FUNDAMENTAL PROPERTIES

BACKGROUND

- » The preceding lectures all build up to the fifteen fundamental properties
- » Some of the properties will as a result be understood now as mathematically conclusive, practical, and logical
- » The others become easier to accept, and together they form a complete set

MORPHOLOGICAL FEATURES

- » Already derived some structural rules
- » UNIVERSAL SCALING
- » WIDE BOUNDARIES
- » SCALING COHERENCE
- » UNIVERSAL DISTRIBUTION OF SIZES
- » How many such rules are there altogether? Completeness?

INNATE STRUCTURE

- » Morphological features that resonate with the human senses
- » Found in man-made form and structure
- » Independent of culture, period, or region — something innate
- » Also present in natural forms and objects

....

We are computing architectural and urban configurations using a Darwinian process of selection, and the 15 properties are going to be the selection criteria used for making decisions at each point in the computations. I have derived some of them based upon mathematical arguments in the previous lectures, and now proceed to complete the set of properties. Rather than beginning the series of lectures with the 15 Fundamental Properties, I thought it more instructive to derive a few of them as an introduction to the very idea of geometrical and configurational properties. These are not a personal preference of Alexander or myself, and neither are they specific to any particular culture.

....

PRESENTATION

- » Christopher Alexander derived the 15 properties by observing structure that "is alive" in buildings, cities, artifacts
- » Alexander's "The Nature of Order, Book 1: THE PHENOMENON OF LIFE"
- » Explanatory hierarchy: these properties are present in nature; biological forms; animals; human beings; cultures

LIST OF PROPERTIES

» 1. Levels of scale
» 2. Strong centers
» 3. Thick boundaries
» 4. Alternating repetition
» 5. Positive space
» 6. Good shape
» 7. Local symmetries
» 8. Deep interlock and ambiguity

LIST OF PROPERTIES (CONT.)

» 9. Contrast
» 10. Gradients
» 11. Roughness
» 12. Echoes
» 13. The void
» 14. Simplicity and inner calm
» 15. Not-separateness

THE SECOND SET OF LEITNER DIAGRAMS

» Diagrams drawn by Helmut Leitner, a software engineer in Graz, Austria
» Schematic sketches — illustrate the fifteen properties at a glance
» Presented at the 2007 conference entitled "Structure-Process-Patterns" in Vienna
» Leitner's book "Mustertheorie (Pattern Theory)" does NOT contain his diagrams

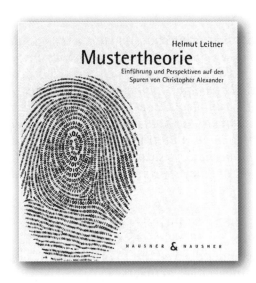

Helmut Leitner's book: „Pattern Theory" (in German)

1. LEVELS OF SCALE

SCALING HIERARCHY

» Repeating components of the same size and similar shape define a scale
» Levels of scale — spaced closely enough for coherence, but not too close to blur the distinction between nearby scales
» Mathematical rules (Lecture 1) for generating the correct scales via the logarithmic constant e and the Fibonacci sequence

ACCESSIBLE SCALING HIERARCHY IS ESSENTIAL FOR ADAPTATION

» The whole point of adaptive design is to satisfy needs on the human scales
» There is an entire range of human scales, from 2 m down to < 1 mm
» Build appropriate form — rule only says that you must accommodate all these scales; shape depends on centers!

2. STRONG CENTERS

•

THEORY OF CENTERS (LECTURE 5)

» Each "center" ties a substantial region of space together coherently
» Each center combines surrounding centers and boundaries to focus
» Centers support each other on every scale — recursive hierarchical property

TWO TYPES OF CENTERS

» Two types of centers — "defined" and "implied" — interact coherently
» "Defined" center has something in the middle to focus attention
» "Implied" center has a boundary that focuses attention on its empty interior
» Visual focus enhances function, precondition for the use of spaces

3. THICK BOUNDARIES

THICK BOUNDARY AS AN "IMPLIED" CENTER

» According to universal scaling, thick boundary arises as the next scale
» Thin boundaries are ineffective, because they skip over one or more terms in the scaling hierarchy, so the boundary is not connected to what it bounds
» The concept of THICK BOUNDARY is important enough to use as a separate structural property

"PERFORATED, BENT, AND FOLDED" (LECTURE 2)

» An "implied" center is defined only through a thick boundary
» Therefore, thick boundaries play a focusing role as well as a bounding role
» Complex semi-permeable urban boundaries must be thick!

4. ALTERNATING REPETITION

INFORMATIONAL DEFINITION

» Essential translational symmetry
» But simplistic repetition is collapsible information
» What repeats is trivially coded (X, repeat 100 times)
» Contrast and repetition reinforce each other through alternation

5. POSITIVE SPACE

REFERS TO GESTALT PSYCHOLOGY

» Ties into the basis of human perception
» Convexity plays a major role in defining an object or a space (area or volume)

- » Mathematical plus psychological reasons
- » Strongly applicable to the spaces we inhabit
- » Threat felt from objects sticking out

POSITIVE BACKGROUND

- » Apply positive space concept to both figure and background
- » Urban space must be positive; not only the building's interior space
- » Ignoring this property ruined most urban spaces built in the 20th century

6. GOOD SHAPE

GOOD SHAPE

- » Symmetries reduce information overload
- » Perceivable objects produce a represented shape from 2-D views, which the brain can computationally manipulate in 3-D
- » "Good" means "easily graspable" — brain's innate need to compactify information
- » Shapes not easily represented strain the computation, hence induce anxiety

7. LOCAL SYMMETRIES

SYMMETRIES WITHIN HIERARCHY

- » Within universal scaling, symmetries must act on every scale
- » "Symmetry" does not mean overall symmetry, as is usually envisioned
- » We have multiple subsymmetries acting within larger symmetries
- » Hierarchically nested symmetries

8. DEEP INTERLOCK AND AMBIGUITY

INTERLOCK

- » Another strong way of connecting
- » Forms interpenetrate to link together
- » Analogy comes from fractals, where lines tend to fill portions of space, and surfaces grow with accretions
- » Abrupt transition does not bind objects coming up to each other

"PERFORATED, BENT, AND FOLDED"

- » Geometrical concept introduced earlier (Lecture 2)
- » Two regions interpenetrate at a semi-permeable interface
- » Because interface enables transition, ambiguity as to which side of the interface one belongs while inside the transition region

9. CONTRAST

CONTRAST IS NECESSARY:

- » A. To establish distinct subunits
- » B. To distinguish between adjoining units
- » C. To provide figure-ground symmetry of opposites
- » False transparency reduces contrast
- » Reduced contrast weakens design

USES OF CONTRAST

- » Space under an arcade versus open street space
- » Strongly contrasted, yet strongly connected
- » Weak spaces: inside versus outside a glass curtain wall — no contrast
- » Use contrast with interlock

10. GRADIENTS

GRADIENTS = TRANSITIONS

» Getting away from uniformity, because it is non-adaptive
» Subdivision does that, but...
» — sometimes we should not quantize form into discrete pieces, but need to change it gradually
» Urban transect: city to countryside
» Interior spaces: public to private

11. ROUGHNESS

MANY DIFFERENT MANIFESTATIONS OF ROUGHNESS — ALL POSITIVE!

» A. Fractal structure goes all the way down in scales — nothing is smooth
» B. Relaxation of strict geometry to allow imperfections — more tolerant
» C. Ornament can be interpreted as "roughness" in a smooth geometry

ROUGHNESS AND SYMMETRY BREAKING

» So-called "imperfections" differentiate repeated units to make them similar but not identical — hand-painted tiles
» Symmetry breaking (approximate) prevents informational collapse
» Deliberate roughness in repetition

ROUGHNESS AND ADAPTATION

» Sustainability implies adaptation
» Local conditions create roughness — breaks regularity and perfect symmetry
» The whole changes during computation according to its context, thus it becomes unique
» HIERARCHY: sustainability; adaptivity; uniqueness; roughness

12. ECHOES

TWO TYPES OF ECHOES:

- » A. Translational symmetry — similar forms found on the same scale but at a distance
- » B. Scaling symmetry — similar forms exist at different scales
- » All natural fractals obey fractal similarity — not exactly similar when magnified, but only "echoes"

13. THE VOID

LARGEST SCALE OF FRACTAL

- » Largest open component of a fractal survives as the void
- » Not possible to fill in all of a fractal with detail
- » In "implied" centers, a complex boundary focuses on the open middle — the void

14. SIMPLICITY AND INNER CALM

MORE SUBTLE QUALITY

- » Lack of clutter — a separate property
- » Balance achieved by overall coherence
- » Symmetries all cooperating to support each other — nothing extraneous or distracting
- » Appears effortless (though such coherence is in fact very difficult to achieve)

SIMPLICITY IN NATURE

- » Never actually "simple" in the sense of being minimalist

» "Simple" in nature means extremely complex but highly coherent
» A system appears "simple" to us because it is so perfect; the form is seamless

15. NOT-SEPARATENESS

ACHIEVING COHERENCE

» Coherence is an emergent property — not present in the individual components
» In a larger coherent whole, no piece can be taken away
» Decomposition is neither obvious, nor possible

MEASURE OF COHERENCE

» When every component is cooperating to give a coherent whole, nothing looks separate, nothing draws attention
» This is the goal of adaptive design
» A seamless blending of an enormous number of complex components
» The opposite of willful separateness

EXTENDING OUTSIDE

» Not-separateness goes beyond internal coherence
» The whole connects to its environment
» Connects with everything beyond itself
» Try as much as possible to generate large-scale coherence

BREAKING THE 15 PROPERTIES FOR FUN

» 15 properties give coherent form, which is so natural that it is hardly noticed — like nature!
» Architects and students most often wish to draw attention to their designs
» Draw attention by violating the 15 properties
» But doing so causes physiological anxiety for user

MORAL QUANDARY

» Do I follow the 15 properties to design an adaptive, nourishing environment?
» Or do I deliberately break them and design an eye-catching project?

» Is playing with emotions (especially anxiety) likely to promote my work?
» What does the client demand?

SUPPRESSION OF THE 15 PROPERTIES

» Whether consciously or unconsciously, architectural design in the 20th century has cultivated the absence of the 15 properties
» Students and architects respond emotionally (very negatively) to them, from their image-based conditioning

NOW ARCHITECTS HAVE A CHOICE

» **The 15 properties question the validity of the contemporary built environment, and the ideology that gave rise to it**
» Weak arguments support forms that violate the 15 properties
» Emotionally nourishing coherence, reflected in all traditional architectures, is both logical and inevitable

Human beings, with their evolved physiology and perception mechanisms, are the most perfectly-tuned instruments for detecting the presence or absence of the 15 properties. At this time, however, architecture critics and architectural academics value forms that violate the 15 properties. The paradigmatic "good" architecture in a contemporary style clashes with the 15 properties. When Alexander or I discuss the 15 properties, they are immediately perceived as contradicting the dominant architectural aesthetic, and are dismissed as irrelevant to design. The fact that they are supported by massive scientific research does not convince architects. Persons trained to value a certain "look" cannot be forced to admit that the dominant style generates psychological and physiological anxiety. Our genuinely good examples are judged because they provide emotional nourishment, which is found primarily in traditional construction and artifacts.

6.2. THREE LAWS OF ARCHITECTURE

RULE COMPRESSION

» Can we find a reduced basis that includes most of the 15 properties?
» "A Theory of Architecture" argues by analogy with physical processes
» My own complementary approach — reinforces without in any way trying to substitute for the 15 properties

LAW 1. ORDER ON THE SMALLEST SCALE

» Established by paired contrasting elements
» Pairs create balanced visual tension
» Elementary particles with opposite characteristics couple — positive and negative charges, opposite spin states, opposite isospin states, etc.
» Pairwise binding on subatomic, atomic, and molecular levels, all on the short scale

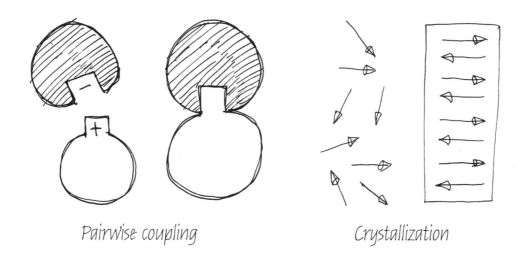

Pairwise coupling   Crystallization

LAW 2. ORDER ON THE LARGE SCALE

» Elements relate to each other at a distance
» Configuration tries to reduce entropy (disorder) by shedding randomness
» Physical fields reduce energy by alignment
» Magnets align along field lines
» Crystallization reduces entropy
» Long-range forces imply ordering

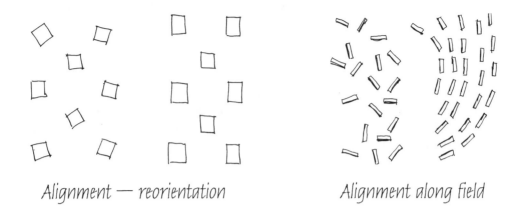

Alignment — reorientation   *Alignment along field*

LAW 3. LINKS SMALL TO LARGE SCALE

» Linking occurs through a regular scaling hierarchy
» Universal scaling with factor $e = 2.7$
» Scales from the largest to the smallest are related by the same scaling ratio
» Already discussed in Lecture 1

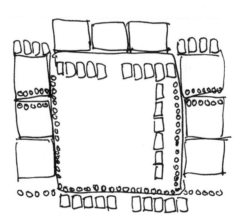

Scaling hierarchy in plan of urban space

The small-scale structures remind us of the small structures inserted into historic urban spaces: street furniture; coffee tables put just outside the restaurants located on the perimeter of the urban space; umbrellas; statues to the heroes of the revolution; benches; some planters with bushes; etc. In a modernist conception, all of this small-scale structure would be considered as superfluous clutter and eliminated, leaving a hard empty plaza. There is no place for a scaling hierarchy in the modernist design idiom.

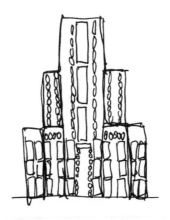

Scaling hierarchy in building façade

Some of the original American skyscrapers, such as those by Louis Sullivan and the Flatiron building by Daniel Burnham, have precisely this hierarchy of scales, which is what makes them so beloved to residents and tourists. They have many structural subdivisions rather than following a monotonous single-scaled monolithic structure that was adopted as the modernist design idiom. The universal distribution of sizes requires that the smaller an architectural component is, the more of them there are.

WHICH OF THE 15 PROPERTIES RELATE TO THE FIRST LAW?

» "Alternating repetition" — repetition of contrasting pairs, not of single unit
» "Deep interlock and ambiguity" — local coupling occurs through geometrical interlock
» "Contrast" — the basis for coupling of units having opposite qualities

WHICH OF THE 15 PROPERTIES RELATE TO THE SECOND LAW?

» "Local symmetries" — disorder is reduced by local symmetries
» "Echoes" — similarity at a distance reduces entropy
» "Not-separateness" — field effect ties components together on different scales

WHICH OF THE 15 PROPERTIES RELATE TO THE THIRD LAW?

» "Levels of scale" — consequence of scaling hierarchy
» "Thick boundaries" — boundary is next-smallest scale in hierarchy
» "The void" — largest scale in hierarchy exists to balance all the smaller scales

CONCLUSION

» Alexander's 15 fundamental properties are an incredibly essential set of practical design tools
» Arguments based on mathematics, physics, chemistry, and biology
» Architects have to accept them as universal, deciding on stylistic reasons whether to follow them or not

CONCLUSION (CONT.)

» Traditional practitioners intuitively recognize some of the 15 properties as part of their own design method
» Yet, some are unknown to them
» Now put together into a coherent set
» I find it more useful to introduce them after having derived basic design rules

LECTURE 7:
ALGORITHMS, FORM LANGUAGE,
AND MEMORY.

7.1. BIOLOGICALLY-INSPIRED COMPUTATION.

7.2. GENETIC ALGORITHMS.

7.3. COMPUTATION VERSUS MEMORY RETRIEVAL.

7.4. EVOLUTIONARY REGRESSION.

7.1. BIOLOGICALLY-INSPIRED COMPUTATION.

BIOLOGICAL FORM IS COMPUTED

» An algorithm that follows or mimics biological processes
» Computation guided by biological constraints towards adaptivity
» Algorithm uses biological sensors to endow the configuration with "life"

PROCESS OF OPTIMIZATION

» Biological systems optimize themselves via selection
» What is being optimized is either physical form, or behavior, or both
» Evolution is therefore a computation with bio-geometrical constraints on the underlying structure

EXAMPLE: LAYING OUT THE PLAN OF A NEW BUILDING

» Suppose we are going to build on a green site, or on an existing lot
» Walk the lot and identify the centers
» Totally emotional, not mathematical
» Use sensory feedback to fit building components into the site
» Influenced by every detail already there

BEST INITIAL FIT

» Match typological elements "entry", "main rooms", "windows", etc. with where emotion and intuition tells us they belong
» Compute the project's morphology using cognitive resonance — using our own body's exquisite biological sensors
» Mark the site with sticks, flags on posts, cardboard panels, chalk on ground, etc.

The configuration is being worked out on the ground itself. It is the result of a recursive process so that we can go back and re-adjust or revise previous steps. New Urbanists use the word "charrette" to mean an off-site participatory discussion, but I mean here the totally different charrette carried out on the site, where the results of the design process are marked on the site. In an off-site charrette everyone will have a different opinion, and the only way a result is reached is through guidance by the more practical architect leading the charrette. But if a group of people is making design decisions on site, they will invariably reach consensus.

PARTICIPATORY DESIGN

» These steps are more accurate when taken with the participation of a group of people — an on-site charrette
» Architects working together with eventual users make decisions ON THE SITE
» Reach a consensus about shapes, paths, placements, and configuration

RADICAL PROPOSITIONS

» A. Consider everything existing on the site — don't just wipe everything clean
» B. Make value judgments about which existing elements are life-enhancing
» C. Save those and discard the rest
» Decide to keep a tree, a large rock, but remove some earth and older structures

PREPARING THE PLAN

» Tens of millions bits of information influence the plan subconsciously!
» Less information available in the office
» **The entire building, or set of buildings, is conceived on the site**
» When on-site design is finished, measure the physical markers on the site to accurately draw the first plan

METHOD AS FORMULATED BY NILI PORTUGALI (TEL-AVIV, ISRAEL)

» Adaptive design method used by Christopher Alexander and his students
» Building grows out of the site, and is not imposed upon the site
» Plan is first encoded on the site itself
» — using low-tech markers and props!

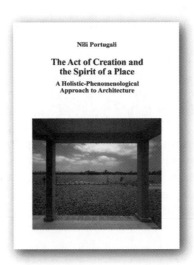

„The Act of Creation and the Spirit of a Place"

STEP 1

»   Identify the main centers of the site:
»   — focal points of geometry
»   — focal points of activity
»   These centers reinforce each other
»   Imagine performing each activity in the building already erected — where does it feel to be the best spot for it?

STEP 2

»   Identify the main and secondary entrances to the site
»   Establish the most natural connection to the existing surroundings: roads, buildings, etc.
»   Use Alexandrine patterns to define approach and entry so that it is enticing

STEP 3

»   Internal paths arise from linking the localized activity centers
»   Sequence: centers first, paths second
»   Define the paths while actually walking on the site
»   Approach from the outside involves one or more paths

STEP 4

»   Decide on the rough boundaries of each center of activity
»   Those boundaries are now beginning to fix the geometry of the plan
»   Choose the entry point for each center
»   This determines the path structure more accurately

STEP 5

»   Decide where to place structures
»   Structures are there to accommodate the activity and geometrical centers, not the other way around!
»   The most intrusive structures go up in the least attractive parts of the site: Alexander's Pattern 104, "SITE REPAIR"

STEP 6

»   Stake out the useful urban space
»   Decide outdoor activities: walking on a path; sitting outside — and reinforce them
»   Coherent urban space is defined by walls, and is not just external left-over space
»   Chapter 2 of "Principles of Urban Structure" — 20C ruined urban space!

It is difficult to find a working urban space, inviting one to stay, created in the past several decades. They are most often hostile and dysfunctional; hence they are never used. We have forgotten how to create urban spaces, and surprisingly so, because there are simple rules to follow. Urban space is defined by a sense of semi-enclosure, and thus depends just as much on the surrounding structures and façades as on the geometry of the space itself. The open space must be defined very carefully so that it is life-enhancing, containing activities and centers, giving it as much attention and delicacy as needs to be given to designing interior spaces. The outside space is dual to the inside space, and each enhances the other.

STEP 7

- » Lay out the future indoor spaces
- » Use all the appropriate patterns from Alexander's "A Pattern Language"
- » Finally, only now decide on the walls!
- » Once this preliminary work has been done, proceed to develop the building

UNEXPECTED FORM

- » What are the indications of success towards an adaptive design?
- » Examined back in the office, the plan feels RIGHT, and it also looks rather UNEXPECTED — a positive quality
- » This means that it is an evolved design, but not an imposed design
- » Could not have been made up

"UNEXPECTED" BUT NOT "ABSURD"

- » I distinguish between our unexpected designs and the absurd forms of contemporary architecture made to shock
- » Evolved design in perfectly adapted, not made up arbitrarily!
- » Absurd forms do not adapt to anything, not even to the program brief!

PROCEED INTO DESIGN

- » Make a list of the project's relevant socio-geometric patterns from Alexander's "A Pattern Language"
- » Derive new patterns needed by the project, if those are not yet developed
- » Look to precedent, tradition, successful solutions under similar circumstances, "the most wonderful and life-enhancing solution to this specific design problem", then adapt it to the project at hand.

THEN COMBINE THE PATTERNS

» Combinatoric method from Chapter 8 of "Principles of Urban Structure"
» Combine patterns acting on smaller scales together hierarchically into higher-level patterns
» Link all scales together through the patterns acting on different scales
» Do not privilege the largest scale!

PROCEED INTO DESIGN (CONT.)

» Decide on your form language
» Tectonic and ornamental vocabulary
» Adopt a pre-existing form language suited to the locality (memory), or create your own form language
» Make sure to use a rich form language — otherwise design cannot be adaptive

CALIBRATE THE FORM LANGUAGE

» Chapter 11 of "A Theory of Architecture" shows that a rich form language will never contradict the pattern language! (Otherwise, discard)
» Express all tectonic elements in the chosen form language
» Pay special attention to smallest scales

....

The form language tells you that tectonic components are of a certain size, using certain materials, and a particular type of developed ornamentation (all of your choice). Every geographical and cultural region will have a totally distinct form language, yet every evolved traditional form language meshes with the Pattern Language, because both languages share a rich and complex linguistic structure. In many cases, architects have adopted a very poor form language made up of stylistic rules that have a minimal internal linguistic structure. For this reason it will never match to the Pattern Language. Drawing the wrong conclusion from this blatant mismatch, ideologically-driven architects have unfortunately thrown out the Pattern Language instead of realizing that their form language is fundamentally flawed.

....

NOW DESIGN THE BUILDING

» Follow recursive rules for creating centers (Lecture 5)
» Previous sequence of seven steps for laying out the ground plan reflects the general approach on all scales
» Adaptive emotion-based computation continues all the way down to the smallest scales of ornamentation

7.2. GENETIC ALGORITHMS

AN ALGORITHM THAT EVOLVES

» An algorithm is a list of instructions
» An algorithm can evolve using a Darwinian processes that selects for success
» Start with an algorithm that works
» Introduce random variations in the code
» Millions of new variants won't work
» One variant may work, and could be better than the original algorithm

MONSTERS FROM GENETIC ALGORITHMS

» Darwinian process of selection can indeed generate monsters — Chapter 10 of "A Theory of Architecture"
» Occurs when you select forms for "cuteness" or "strangeness", not for adaptivity to human needs
» Is the system evolving towards a higher intelligence, or into a monster?

THE KEY HERE IS SELECTION

» In contemporary architecture, selection is usually based on generating forms that induce anxiety!
» Anxiety is misinterpreted as the thrill of exciting new forms, but it actually affects our body negatively
» Adaptive design solutions don't give the same thrill that triggers anxiety (adrenalyne boost, fight-or-flight syndrome)

SELECTION IN DESIGN

» My friends and I apply selection criteria based on human needs and sensibilities — result generates a feeling of wellbeing
» Our selection criteria are the following adaptive CONSTRAINTS (Lecture 5):
» — pattern languages; universal scaling; universal distribution; centers; fifteen fundamental properties, etc.

INCOMPREHENSIBLE COMPLEXITY

» Computer scientist W. Daniel (Danny) Hillis has bred sorting algorithms
» These genetic algorithms are faster than any written by human programmers
» HILLIS DOES NOT UNDERSTAND HOW THEY WORK!
» Their complexity is as long as themselves

This is an example of computational irreducibility. The description of an irreducibly complex system (e.g. the algorithms evolved by Hillis) is as complex as the system itself, so there is no shortcut to understanding how the system works. This is different from a system whose construction and internal function follow human logic, which can be very easily understood. Computational irreducibility is a feature of many evolved designs, whether in biology, computer science, architecture, or urbanism. Those structures cannot be "designed" in the commonly-understood sense of an architect creating something by inspiration. The best architect today cannot completely understand an evolved traditional building or piece of urban fabric.

COLLECTIVE INTELLIGENCE

» Traditional design methods have evolved through Darwinian processes
» Now stored in built memory as part of the traditional environment
» Their complexity equals their code
» No shortcut to understanding how they work — Chapter 10 of "Principles of Urban Structure"

CORRECTNESS OF TRADITIONAL ARCHITECTURAL AND URBAN TYPOLOGIES

» Evolved solutions — they work even if we don't understand exactly why
» Known to solve all problems of a particular type, and to always give an adaptive solution
» These proven results of evolved algorithms must be preserved for use!

ALGORITHMIC AMBIGUITY

» Let's invent a new design algorithm…
» But just because an algorithm gives output, that does not mean its output represents any valid results
» Results may be nonsensical, or toxic
» Validation criteria must come from OUTSIDE the algorithm itself

RULE OF THUMB

» **Design computations must be validated by checking against EVOLVED SOLUTIONS**
» Traditional design gives results known independently to be correct
» Use these as a check before proceeding to more innovative design problems for the contemporary world

7.3. COMPUTATION VERSUS MEMORY RETRIEVAL

YOU DRAW WHAT YOU REMEMBER

» MY CLAIM: Most design relies upon a stored memory bank
» Even when designers thinks they are being most innovative, subconsciously, they are still drawing upon memory
» It is therefore crucial to have a bank of evolved solutions to draw from!

EXAMPLE: SOME FAMOUS ARCHITECTS

» Ludwig Mies van der Rohe, Daniel Libeskind, and Frank Gehry all have their own very narrow design style
» Each re-cycles the same image-based design elements in every building
» Their claim to "innovation" occurred in the very beginning — after that, they rely upon their stored vocabulary

PROCESS OF MEMORY RETRIEVAL

» A trivial mathematical explanation
» Previous results of computations using an algorithm are stored in memory
» Table of products lists entries in a 2-D array
» Look up the result — no computation involved, only recall
» For example, 3 x 5 = 15

X	1	2	3	4	5
1	1	2	3	4	5
2	2	4	6	8	10
3	3	6	9	12	15
4	4	8	12	16	20
5	5	10	15	20	25

Multiplication table

MEMORY IS LIABLE TO CORRUPTION

» Using two coordinates, locate product in memory array: (3, 5) = 15
» But informational virus can invade the memory bank
» Virus replaces data with copies of itself
» Virus uses memory to propagate — computations that rely only on memory make copies of the virus

X	1	2	3	4	5
1	5	5	5	5	5
2	5	5	5	5	5
3	5	5	5	5	5
4	5	5	5	5	5
5	5	5	5	5	5

Multiplication table corrupted by the data virus „5"

FALSE RESULTS

» Computation accesses the correct data position (cell) in memory
» No algorithm is involved
» But memory is corrupted by virus
» Output is wrong: 3 x 5 = 5

CHECK RESULT BY USING ALGORITHM

» Problem: $S = 3 \times 5$
» Write product as a sum $S = 5 + 5 + 5$
» Add the first two numbers $S = 10 + 5$
» Repeat process until you have only a single number
» $S = 15$
» This is the answer

SET UP THE TWO MEMORY BANKS NEEDED FOR ADAPTIVE DESIGN

» Memory bank 1 contains typology
» Memory bank 2 contains socio-geometrical patterns in the sense of Christopher Alexander
» Set up architectural memory bank 1 — a three-dimensional reference system containing evolved solutions

ARCHITECTURAL MEMORY BANK 1

» First axis is urban density: use the Transect system of Andrés Duany and Elizabeth Plater-Zyberk, labeled T1 (rural) to T6 (high urban density)
» Second axis is world location (which includes a form language): Algeria, South-Eastern USA, Nigeria, Scotland, etc.
» Third axis is functional typology: school, bank, church, apartment building, house, store, factory, etc.

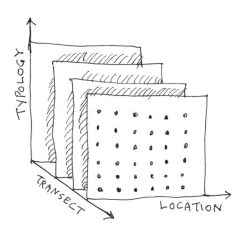

Architectural memory bank 1

URBAN DENSITY: TRANSECT SYSTEM

» Classification of different urban density
» T1 = natural (nature preserve)
» T2 = rural (farmhouses)
» T3 = sub-urban (mixed-use, not sprawl!)
» T4 = general urban (small town)
» T5 = urban center (dense urban fabric)
» T6 = urban core (the densest part of cities)

WORLD LOCATION: LOCAL CULTURE, CLIMATE & MATERIALS

» Form language — language of building developed alongside spoken language

» Evolved via trial-and-error over many years and fine-tuned by generations of users and builders
» Form expression of typologies shaped by culture, climate, local materials

ARCHITECTURAL MEMORY BANK 2

» The Alexandrine pattern data base — separate memory bank solely for patterns
» Universal architectural pattern typologies
» Largely independent of culture, climate, local materials
» Correct solutions depend upon geometry, evolved along with human physiology

ADAPTIVE DESIGN THAT DRAWS FROM EVOLVED MEMORY BANKS

» Define your project in terms of a specific coordinate in 3-D memory
» (x, y, z) = (Transect of urban density, world location, functional typology)
» Look up the unique address in Memory 1
» Recall the relevant patterns for use from Memory 2, then design adaptively

....

It may seem revolutionary to talk about relying upon memory banks containing tried-and-true methods, form languages, and traditional techniques for architecture and urbanism. And I am proposing not one memory bank, but two of them containing distinct types of derived information! All of this was supposedly thrown out with the great innovation of the Bauhaus at the beginning of the 20th Century. Nevertheless, what actually happened is that the evolved memory banks were merely replaced with a new set (a very narrow and non-adaptive stylistic vocabulary). The new memory bank is now used to draw upon, just as before, and that is why the vast majority of buildings in the last several decades tend to look the same. Despite all the rhetoric about innovation, you cannot design without drawing (subconsciously) from a memory bank.

....

HEALTHY EVOLUTION OF ARCHITECTURAL MEMORY BANK 1

» Solutions can change over time
» One typology can merge into another
» Urban density usually changes in time
» Underlying culture in the same place changes, influenced by others
» Solutions adapt to changing conditions

CORRUPTION OF MEMORY BANKS!

» Viruses invade architectural memory 1 and substitute for the architectural data cells
» Memory bank 1 entries now contain only glass or concrete cubes

- » All buildings, in any urban density, all over the world, simply replicate the virus
- » Pattern memory bank 2 is wiped out — erased because it is a viral antibody!

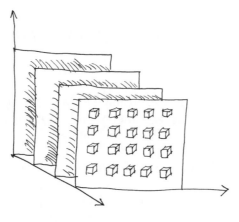

Architectural cube virus

If you apply Patterns in design, they act as viral antibodies to protect from architectural viruses. The ability to mesh a form language into the Pattern Language is a crucial test for the validity of that form language. A made-up, style-based design method is not rich enough to define a form language. For this reason, architects who use viral methods of design take care never to legitimize Alexandrine patterns, since those undo their design method. The common excuse given is that Alexandrine patterns "inhibit creativity", but the correct statement is that the patterns identify viral methods of design which are disguised as "creative". This is the principal reason why the Pattern Language is not routinely taught in design schools today.

NON-ADAPTIVE RESULT FROM CORRUPTED MEMORY BANK 1

- » Go to position (x, y, z) = (T2-rural, eastern Pakistan, schoolhouse)
- » Memory cell is glass and concrete box
- » Go to position (x, y, z) = (T5-urban center, coastal Japan, apartment)
- » Memory cell is glass and concrete box
- » But result is not adaptive to either task!

THE NEED FOR ADAPTIVE ALGORITHMS

- » Architects should apply algorithms that adapt structure to human needs
- » Simple algorithms connect pattern languages to form languages
- » Process successfully generates adaptive design, and corrects irrelevant forms that have corrupted memory

USE AN ALGORITHM, OR MEMORY?

» Use a proven memory bank that archives evolved solutions
» Often just as good as computing a new solution
» When architectural memory banks are corrupted, however, we need to re-compute the solutions all over again
» Pattern languages prevent corruption

The design method proposed here is still based on computations, and the memory banks that I discuss only help to narrow down and facilitate the computational process. Usually, an evolved design solution is adaptive, and will save a large number of steps in the computation. Essentially, an evolved solution stores a number of computational steps that do not have to be repeated each time, only varied to fit the existing context. I am certainly not advocating the mindless re-use of standard typologies, but I emphasize that this is exactly what is practiced today in contemporary building. The same glass-and-steel and concrete boxes (or sprawling ranch-style suburban houses) are erected throughout the world, oblivious of their failings as human environments, mismatch with local culture, and intrinsic unsustainability. This widespread practice is ideologically-driven, and represents the rejection of both computational design and the re-use of evolved solutions.

7.4. EVOLUTIONARY REGRESSION

LOSING HARD-WON FEATURES

» It is very easy to evolve a system backwards, thus reversing its development
» Simply reverse the selection criteria, and a Darwinian process takes care of the rest — it is still adaptation!

THE BLIND MEXICAN CAVEFISH *ASTYANAX*

» Fish originally lived outside caves, and evolved a well-developed eye
» Its outside relatives have good eyes
» *Astyanax* in caves has lost its eyes
» Backwards evolutionary adaptation to light-less cave environment

JAN MICHL (OSLO, NORWAY)

» Most design is in fact redesign
» A sequence of corrections, additions, modifications, improvements, refinements

- » Adaptive design of artifacts is quintessentially Darwinian
- » Selection is a "process of tinkering"
- » Design as innovation is only a myth

EVOLUTION OF TOOLS AND ARTIFACTS

- » Designers never begin from a clean slate
- » Function depends upon existing form
- » The slogan "form follows function" really means "form follows purpose"
- » The formalist purpose is simply to impose new criteria for selection

FUNCTION NEVER PRECEDES FORM!

- » The purpose of Bauhaus designers was to promote a palette of industrial materials and a narrow stylistic vocabulary of sleek, shiny forms
- » Unconcerned with the actual function of artifacts, buildings, or cities
- » Modernist designers validated their purpose by referring to fictive demands of the "Spirit of the Age"

MORE BY JAN MICHL

- » "The modernist artistic visions were inflicted on the captive audience of the socially weak sections of the population" — no selection there!
- » Governments and the media embraced the allure of the avant-garde
- » We adopted the non-adapted modernist style because it was IMPOSED on us!

In the 1920s and 1930s, governments were seduced by the political promises of the Bauhaus and sponsored innovative and often monstrous new building typologies. The Bauhaus and its ideological successors wrote voluminous propaganda to justify their narrow purpose, and these publicity efforts used attractive slogans to deceive the world into believing that evolutionary "progress" was being offered. That's false. While industrial materials and construction techniques contained some elements of progress, the style being offered was an evolutionary regression. Monstrous social housing projects and skyscrapers express a totemic design that is part of a formalist statement. We adopted the non-adaptive modernist style because it was imposed on us. Worse than that, this style is totally unsustainable.

FORWARD EVOLUTION OF BOOKS

- » Biological evolution created mechanism of the eye-brain system
- » Typography evolved over several centuries to optimize information transfer
- » — serif fonts (Times); black ink; matte soft-white paper; 12 point font size, etc.

» Minimizes the brain-information interface
» Maximizes information transfer rate

BACKWARDS EVOLUTION OF ARCHITECTURE BOOKS

» **Use sans-serif fonts (Helvetica)**
» Use light gray instead of black ink
» Use too small a font size (9-10 point)
» Use highly glossy paper — too reflective to focus on
» Use unusual page formatting to show off fashionable typographic "style"

EASE OF READING IS DEGRADED

» No paragraph breaks — confusion of textual and logical subdivision!
» No paragraph indents — ugly!
» Photos are intentionally blurred!
» Yet, these negative characteristics have proliferated — they define a highly successful ANTIPATTERN

SELECTION OVER A FEW DECADES

» The Bauhaus style introduced sans-serif fonts with the "machine aesthetic"
» Selection criteria imposed by architects, authors, publishers, and a public fascinated with the "new look"
» Style takes precedence over legibility
» Obvious in recent architecture books

ONE EXAMPLE AMONG MANY

» One recent book ("Choral Works") on architectural theory by a world-famous architect, co-authored with a world-famous philosopher, has holes punched in it!
» Book is intentionally illegible
» Highly praised, and recommended as course textbook in our elite universities

ARCHITECTURAL IMAGES HAVE ALSO EVOLVED BACKWARDS

» Architectural renderings as vague translucent screen shots — no detail
» One cannot grasp the overall forms
» "Competition project style" combines reflective with transparent surfaces
» But their optical properties prevent the eye from focusing — cannot see them!

ANOTHER EXAMPLE AMONG MANY

» Lectures by a world-famous architect ("Santiago Calatrava: Conversations with Students — The MIT Lectures")
» Illustrated with blurry monochrome brown photos of the famous architect, intentionally made grainy
» Book would probably not sell if the photos were clear and focused!
» Only the fashionable "style" sells

INFORMATION OBTAINED ONLY THROUGH PAIN

» Contemporary architecture books intentionally or unintentionally strain the eyes of the reader
» Yet students have to study them for their courses
» Is this regression an oversight, or is it causing pain to reinforce power?

CONCLUSIONS

» Algorithmic design that is adaptive relies upon emotion — uses the human computer
» Architecture schools teach rationalization for each design decision — but that's not computational!
» It is really the rationalization of a style
» True computation results in unusual and unexpected (not "absurd") configurations

LECTURE 8:
INHUMAN ARCHITECTURE
AND ARCHITECTURAL EDUCATION.

8.1. EMERGENT SYSTEMS.

8.2. EXAMPLES FROM ARTIFICIAL LIFE.

8.3. INHUMAN EXPERIMENTS.

8.4. ARCHITECTURAL EDUCATION.

8.1. EMERGENT SYSTEMS

PREAMBLE

» Notice that current architectural education and practice are opposite to the method presented in my lectures
» But established system is not integral with natural and biological systems
» If we want sustainability, my lectures provide the most helpful direction

SOCIAL CONTAGION

» I now apply systems theory to explain some phenomena of human society
» Systems develop new characteristics not present in the initial inputs — an instance of EMERGENCE
» A system of beliefs grows over time, and eventually takes over a society
» Social contagion spreads a new norm

POWER AS AN EMERGENT PHENOMENON

» Ideology and questionable beliefs lead to the emergence of a power structure
» System grows in strength and detaches itself from the rest of the world
» Becomes more and more insular (to protect itself)
» Periodic "reform" perpetuates power structure — a staged deception

GEORGE ORWELL'S NOVEL "1984"

» The past is erased — people are forced to live in the present
» Power is expressed by inflicting pain
» Reality is defined only by the system
» There is no other truth to turn towards
» Totalitarian system re-writes history

A "NEW" TRADITION EMERGES

» Movement based on ideas turns into an institutional power base
» Irrational ideas are transformed into established (rational!) practice
» Henceforth, the system's goal is simply to perpetuate the existing power structure by any available means

....

The success of such a belief system has nothing to do with the validity of its ideas, but only with the success those ideas have in spreading among the population. That's due as much to fashion and meme propagation as to truth and validity. The ideas themselves could be irrational. But if they are supported

*by the society, and even legalized by the system, then they are followed unques-
tioningly. They become established practice, and by definition, they become "rational". This doomsday picture that George Orwell painted is relevant more than
ever today. I wish to apply these concepts to understand how architectural education has moved away from teaching adaptive design, towards propagating a
peculiar design ideology.*

EDUCATIONAL SYSTEM IGNORES BIOPHILIA AND ADAPTIVITY

» System of architectural education concentrates upon abstract forms
» Style-based design is detached from biological needs and from nature
» Design is detached from spiritual needs
» There is no integrity with humanity

MAIN GOALS FOR ARCHITECTURAL EDUCATION

» Should be to raise people's awareness of the effects of the built environment
» To take responsibility for one's designs
» To focus on wellbeing of inhabitants
» Not only to come up with novel shapes
» Not to become mindless pawns of a manipulative power system

8.2. EXAMPLES FROM ARTIFICIAL LIFE

GOOD AND BAD ASPECTS

» Innocent aspect: pixels on a computer screen move around and gobble each
  other up — only a game
» Alarming aspect: the two-way transformation between living beings and machines — some developments are positive and liberating, but others are negative and extremely serious
» This latter process has re-shaped humanity in the 20th Century

RELATIONSHIP BETWEEN MACHINES AND LIVING BEINGS

» Two possible ways to go:
» A. UP — make machines mimic capabilities of living beings
» B. DOWN — reduce living beings to the characteristics of machines
» Going DOWN determines the form of the 20th Century's built environment

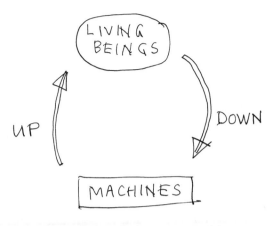

From living being to machine

GOING UP — ENHANCE MACHINES

» Computers enhance our capabilities
» Great successes in robotics: Rodney Brooks' Mars Explorer
» Industrial robots can work in delicate, dangerous, or repetitive conditions
» Military robots save lives — more expendable than humans

GOING UP (CONT.)

» Add more and more intelligent qualities to machines, so that they are able to mimic human capabilities
» Increase their perceptive mechanisms
» Increase their capacity to process information
» Increase autonomous action capability

GOING DOWN — REDUCE BEINGS

» Advertising brainwashes people (Le Corbusier was an advertising pioneer!)
» Manipulate people as inert entities
» Transforms human beings into mechanical consumers of industrial products
» Brainwash humans to act as suicide bombers — expendable beings

GOING DOWN (CONT.)

» Remove more and more intelligent qualities from humans, until they begin to act like machines
» Decrease perceptive mechanisms
» Decrease capacity for processing information
» Decrease autonomous action capability

INDUSTRIALIZATION OF ANIMALS

» Beings become an industrial product
» Battery-raised chickens pass all their lives crammed together in atrocious conditions
» Bred with growth hormones and genetically modified — made into unnatural monsters
» Laboratory animals used in cruel and inhumane experiments

INDUSTRIALIZATION OF PEOPLE

» Mass production driven by speed, volume, efficiency, cost, bottom line
» Uses workers as machines, or as simple cogs in a production machine
» Reduces the complex humanity of people to a single mechanistic function

CONTEMPORARY TRENDS

» French-Canadian philosopher and author Ollivier Dyens explores the merging of humans with machines
» — in his book "Metal and Flesh", MIT Press, Cambridge, 2001
» Major trend underlying all our culture
» More DOWN than UP

„Metal and Flesh"

ARTIFICIAL LIFE

» Was achieved in the 20th Century
» — opposite of what was expected!
» — not the elevation of machines to the level of humans, or even animals
» Instead, the reduction of animals and human beings to the level of machines

SOCIAL ENGINEERING

» Creates monsters from living beings
» Manipulates their genetic information to create unnatural new forms of life
» Seeks to fundamentally re-shape life forms so that they benefit industrial production and consumption
» Aims to fit life into a machine world

THREE LEVELS OF BEING HUMAN (IN DECREASING ORDER)

» 3. The transcendent human being
» 2. The biological human being
» 1. The abstract (mechanical) human being
» Most complete, most fulfilling existence moves through all three levels
» A majority of contemporary architecture and urbanism acts on level 1 — misnamed "rationality"

....

Whether you are religious or not, most people accept the fact that human beings are somehow tied to the complexity of the universe. Established religions are based on the concept that there exists a higher order, and humans come closer to connecting to that higher order than do the other animals. We are sentient, and we have compassion and understanding (in a moral and philosophical sense). We are apparently the only living entity that appreciates the complexity of the universe. This stage of existence defines humanity at level 3. The next lower level is the biological human being, sharing the marvelous complex biology with all other living structures. Humanity at level 2 is still full of wonders that science is only beginning to understand. All the world's great literature and philosophy, up until the 20C, accepts these three levels of humanity.

....

BIOPHILIC DESIGN

» N.A.S. & Kenneth Masden: "Neuroscience, the Natural Environment, and Building Design"
» — Chapter 5 of "Biophilic Design: The Theory, Science, and Practice of Bringing Buildings to Life", Stephen Kellert, Judith Heerwagen & Martin Mador, Editors, Wiley, New York, 2008

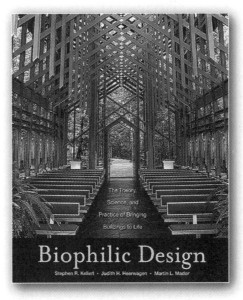

„Biophilic Design"

For example, the cover of our book shows the Thorncrown Chapel by Fay Jones, a contemporary architect who did practice adaptive design and searched for a material connection to the human being and to the sacred. My point is that Jones has remained outside the current list of fashionable architects, and is all but ignored in architecture schools today.

BIOPHILIC ARCHITECTURE RESPECTS HUMAN LEVELS 2 AND 3

» An architecture that focuses on human feelings and psychology
» Architecture concerned primarily with human biology and sensitivities
» Design that never imposes any formal ideas without testing their effects
» Design that rejects social engineering

ARCHITECTS AND INDUSTRIALIZATION

» Architects accept the "machine aesthetic" and its unnatural forms
» Architects are among the most enthusiastic supporters of technological solutions to the built environment
» But they don't notice when certain applications of technology reduce human beings to machines

UTOPIA BECOMES DYSTOPIA

» Hopeful dream of utopia transformed into the nightmare of dystopian despair

» Already recognized by science-fiction authors, but not yet by philosophers
» Culture of architectural despair in the high-rise slums of the French cités and dystopian urban regions the world over

8.3. INHUMAN EXPERIMENTS

DEGRADATION OF HUMANS

» When human beings are degraded to machines, atrocious actions become possible, and even feasible
» Dominant idea of "progress" (as envisioned by social engineers) gets confused with inhuman pursuits
» But this is not true science, because it does not follow the scientific method

HUMAN EXPERIMENTS TODAY

» Carefully regulated by government
» First tried out on laboratory animals
» Only after effects are well understood to be safe, then tried on volunteer human subjects, not forced on people
» If there are any obvious negative signs, the experiment is discontinued

CONTROL GROUP IS ADDITIONAL CHECK

» Experiments on humans are always carried out with a control group
» Continuously compare state of subjects with those in the control group
» If any negative statistical effect is found as compared to the control group, experiment is terminated

A group of people who are not taking part in the experiment (say, receiving an experimental drug or medical treatment) are randomly mixed into the trial, and continuously compared with those who are participating. As far as possible, experimenters try to hide who is participating and who is not, so as to avoid psychophysiological effects: i.e., the control works better if those subjects believe they are actually receiving the new drug and not a placebo. If there is a negative statistical divergence between those taking the new drug and those who do not, for any reasons not understood, then the experiment is terminated. This is a separate and very important statistical control.

INHUMAN EXPERIMENTS

» Those that ignore established checks
» Masquerade as "scientific enquiry"
» Unconcerned with fate of the subjects
» Experimenter declares noble intention: "to solve the problems of humanity"
» Most often, experiments are carried out with detachment and indifference

DOUBLE STANDARD FOR HUMAN EXPERIMENTS

» The medical industry is held to strict standards for human experimentation
» But architects and urbanists experiment freely on millions of humans without any controls or supervision
» Even with massive evidence, toxic typologies continue to be marketed and built

LE CORBUSIER

» Pseudonym of Charles-Édouard Jeanneret-Gris
» Designed inhuman environments for millions of persons without ever considering their effects on occupants
» Very creative in proposing far-ranging ideas for building and city form

ABSOLUTE SELF-ASSURANCE

» Le Corbusier was convinced of the absolute truth and moral value of his own inspiration
» Never questioned the correctness of his schemes, but treated them as revealed wisdom (religious presumption)
» Le Corbusier's ideas were never tested
» But they are applied repeatedly!

LE CORBUSIER'S POINTS

» 1. Architecture of the horizontal (Lecture 2)
» 2. Anti-gravity anxiety (Lecture 2)
» 3. Overhanging slabs (Lecture 2)
» 4. Flat or tilted plane ceilings and roofs
» 5. Randomization of tectonic forms
» 6. Rough exterior materials for indoor surfaces — brutalist concrete

LE CORBUSIER'S POINTS (CONT.)

» 7. Forbid ornament (taken from Adolf Loos)
» 8. Banish complex and natural colors

» 9. Force people into high-rise buildings
» 10. Disconnect families from nature
» 11. Disconnect children from the earth
» 12. Destroy urban space by gigantism
» 13. Erase the human scale of streets

INHUMAN ARCHITECTURE

» Le Corbusier invented a vocabulary of forms, all of which provoke anxiety
» Used as standard design typologies
» Their brilliant effectiveness and consistency cannot be accidental
» Le Corbusier defined a "rational" world based upon psychological anxiety

----

A growing group of writers has finally exposed Le Corbusier for what he really was. Evidently, the distance of time has broken down the aura of untouchability that has in the past cloaked him in a sacred mantle. "Le Corbusier was to architecture what [Cambodian dictator and mass-murderer] Pol Pot was to social reform … He turned his gifts to destructive ends, and it is no coincidence that he willingly served both Stalin and Vichy. Like Pol Pot, he wanted to start from Year Zero: before me, nothing; after me, everything … When one recalls Le Corbusier's remark about reinforced concrete —"my reliable, friendly concrete"— one wonders if he might have been suffering from a degree of Asperger's syndrome … Le Corbusier's hatred of the human went well beyond words, of course." — Theodore Dalrymple, City Journal, Autumn 2009.

HOSPITALS AND APARTMENT BLOCKS

» Le Corbusier planned a hospital for Venice with no windows
» From biophilia, we know that healing environments absolutely require sunlight and views of nature
» *Unité d'Habitation* in France — apartment block with extra-thin walls create terrible noise problem; terrible glare from the windows; the elevators stop only on every other floor

RELIGIOUS ARCHITECT?

» Commissioned by Father Marie-Alain Couturier, who regarded Le Corbusier as "the greatest living architect"
» 1. Convent of Sainte-Marie de la Tourette, France, 1953 (actually by Iannis Xenakis)
» 2. Chapel of Notre-Dame du Haut, Ronchamp, France, 1956
» 3. Church of Saint-Pierre de Firminy, France, completed only in 2006

» Le Corbusier eagerly participated in the competition to build the "Palace of the Soviets" in Moscow in 1931
» Project was under Josef Stalin's personal encouragement
» Site was cleared by dynamiting the glorious "Cathedral of Christ the Savior", a perfectly sound building

Architecture of the sacred?

I have witnessed fanaticism whenever Le Corbusier is criticized in architectural circles. Educated, rational, cultured persons begin to act irrationally and sometimes violently. This reaction reveals their basic belief system to be aligned with the teachings of Le Corbusier in a religious sense. Unfortunately, and despite all evidence to the contrary, this deification of Le Corbusier feeds the myth of his being a great church architect.

"WE MUST KILL THE STREET!"

» — Le Corbusier quoted by Sybil Moholy-Nagy, "Matrix of Man: An Illustrated History of Urban Environment", Praeger, New York, 1968, page 274
» Was obsessed with erasing street life and daily human interaction
» Are Le Corbusier's ideas an expression of his psychological problems?

"Corbusier's criminally insane Plan Voisin, Paris: thank God the architects weren't in charge... [He] proposed razing the organic street pattern of the entire Marais district in Paris and replacing it with a half baked neo-fascist masterplan, the product of excessive ego." — Affordable Housing Institute, 9 August 2009. "The main criticism of Le Corbusier, reiterated without fatigue for more than seventy years, has been that he forgot cities exist to facilitate socializing. Some commentators have gone further: Le

Corbusier was not simply negligent or naive but sick, perhaps mad." — Simon Richards, Common Knowledge 13:1, 2007, pages 51-52.

THE FATE OF "PINCEAU"

» Was Le Corbusier's favorite dog
» After Pinceau died, Le Corbusier had the skin used to bind his favorite book
» He bound Cervantes' "Don Quixote" in Pinceau's fur
» Catherine de Smet, "Le Corbusier, Architect of Books", Lars Müller Publishers, Baden, Switzerland, 2006

INHUMAN URBANISM

» Le Corbusier was pathologically obsessed with destroying traditional urban fabric
» Collaborated with the Nazi-supported Vichy regime, urging Marshal Pétain to destroy Algiers during the war
» He finally convinced the post-war French occupation authority to do it

Marshal Pétain despised Le Corbusier, and refused even to meet with him. In any case, the Vichy regime was too busy with the war to do anything with Algiers. It is surprising, however, that so many of the persons who openly collaborated with the German occupation of France were tried and shot after the end of the war while Le Corbusier, who held an official position with the state urbanist department of the Vichy government, managed to come out unscathed as a high-ranking great architect. "Le Comité d'Études Préparatoires Urbaniques" was formed in 1939 by Le Corbusier and Jean Giraudoux (who had written the introduction to Le Corbusier's Charter of Athens). Giraudoux wrote elsewhere: "We are in full agreement with Hitler in proclaiming that a policy only achieves its highest plane if it is racial". — Nicholas Fox Weber, "Le Corbusier: A Life", Knopf, 2008: page 407.

MODEL FOR URBANICIDE

» In destroying Algiers, Le Corbusier showed a fanatical hostility against traditional Islamic urbanism
» The Arab/Islamic world noticed this, and has never forgiven the West
» Mohamed Atta wrote his thesis on the modernist urban destruction of Aleppo

THE ANGEL OF URBAN DEATH

» Cover of Le Corbusier's book containing his plans for destroying Algiers has a drawing by him of the Angel of Death

» Resembles representations of Satan found in various images from different cultures throughout history

Pazuzu (Iraq, 500BC)

Satan as androgynous goat

Le Corbusier's own hand holding the angel of death over Algiers, adapted from the cover of Le Corbusier's book „Poésie sur Alger", Falaize, Paris, 1950.

THINGS ONLY GOT WORSE

» Contemporary buildings go far beyond Le Corbusier's in producing anxiety
» In the past few decades, we have seen a descent into even more inhuman architectural experiments
» Some new art museums assault the senses, causing nausea and vertigo

NOVEL INHUMAN EXPERIMENTS

» Extend the sensual assault of blank, forbidding concrete or glass walls
» New techniques include: blobs; oozing forms; translucent walls; curvilinear shiny metal surfaces; zigzags; spikes
» All of these tectonic typologies generate user anxiety, but no-one cares

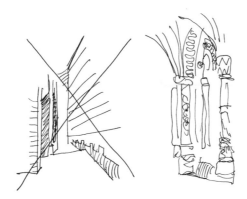

Anxiety-producing versus life-enhancing geometries

MEDIA COLLUSION

» Architecture critics write intelligent (but false) arguments that praise inhuman design experiments
» They use the language of technology to erase human feelings about form and place, disguising or denying the anxiety
» Convince the rest of the world to eagerly import "fashionable" designs

Our generation has willingly chosen to promote and build anxiety-producing buildings, while at the same time destroying what is left of life-enhancing geometries. The media is successful in convincing the rest of the world to import these designs into the remotest regions of the world, and to erase their own architectural traditions. The developing world has been sold the image of anxiety-producing architecture as the key to modernization, and as being essential for social and economic progress.

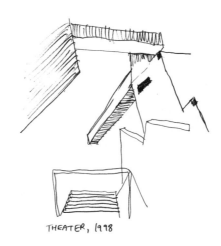

THEATER, 1998

Mapping sadism onto built form

MARKET-DRIVEN PATHOLOGIES

» Our consumer culture is passively masochistic in the face of media and academic authority
» Clients pay good money to live in a building that makes them ill-at-ease
» Museum-goers buy an entrance ticket to feel nauseous in an Art Museum

GLOBAL CAPITAL IN THE SERVICE OF INHUMAN IDEOLOGY

» Discards and erases architectural traditions the world over
» Governments often force this on their people — "for their own good!"
» An aggression towards humanistic traditional architectures, yet many people welcome this as "progress"

Today's global economy drives the creation of monstrous and inhuman environments by following a deeply flawed model. Capital seeking an investment venue finds a ready outlet in speculative construction, and the larger the project, the easier it is to manage the investment. To protect their investment, institutional investors often turn to an already famous architect as insurance. The "name" architect is asked to design something spectacular, confusing the perceived media impact with market value (although we have set bad precedents where the two come together in a deficient product that nevertheless sells to gullible clients). Those architects live only by transcending every architectural precedent and feel absolutely no obligation towards human sensibilities (being influenced only by the modernist ideology of hatred towards traditional architecture). Therefore, their supposed innovation through form and materials is ultimately no more adaptive than the old glass-and-steel or concrete boxes. The design methods presented in this book are irrelevant to projects that play to the media instead of adapting to their inhabitants. The theories discussed here might prove useful only as plagiarized sound bites that dishonestly promote absurd and alien projects designed without any logic. The public does not know any better, and the architectural critics go along with this deception because they are part of the system. A very powerful industry needs to make a return on its investment, so even the most disastrous architectural failures are never admitted publicly. We read about them only decades later.

ARCHITECTURE AS NOURISHMENT

» Morally nourishing architecture through life-enhancing qualities of pattern, color, geometry, rhythm — gives satisfaction for user
» Architecture can also bring out the darkest regions of the human soul: nihilism, schizophrenia, sadism, power — gives satisfaction for architect

STOP INHUMAN EXPERIMENTS!

» Simply require the same standards as with medical human experiments
» But architects are not interested in the effects of their creations — dogma of abstract form still rules
» This development can only be market-driven, therefore educate the clients

8.4. ARCHITECTURAL EDUCATION

TEACH ADAPTIVE DESIGN

» Why are we training our students to design buildings detached from nature?
» I wish to put back the component of integrity into architecture schools
» Re-situate in academia and the media an obligation towards human beings
» Re-orient design in a totally different direction from the spectacular image

Borrowing a term from Roger Scruton, I believe that architectural education has turned from a truth-directed into a power-directed system of thought. "The perfect totalitarian ideology: a pseudo-science that justifies and recruits resentment, that undermines and dismisses all rival claims to legitimacy and that endows the not quite successful with the proof of their superior intellectual power..." — A Political Philosophy, page 153. Scruton is referring to political systems, and I claim that architecture has become one, using the educational system to perpetuate itself. The university administration is complicit, because up until now it supports this system and has allowed a contempt for human life to root itself in academia. As far as the university is concerned, as long as there are students filling up classrooms "everything is fine": it washes its hands of what is actually taught there.

CONTEMPORARY DESIGN

» Architecture schools now teach courses in algorithmic design — a new interest
» But algorithmic design as a purely formal approach creates monsters
» A biophilic worldview guarantees designs integral with natural systems

INHUMAN ALGORITHMIC DESIGN

» Generates anxiety disguised as a celebration of novelty — the search for "playful" abstract forms
» Take "cute" results of a geometrical algorithm and use them to design an inhuman building or urban region
» No human constraints applied — e.g. biophilia, adaptivity, pattern languages

New algorithmic design (unbuilt)

There *are new books on algorithmic design for architecture students being published that will surely compete with this book. I wish to make clear that those authors are talking about entirely different things: namely, the generation of irrelevant forms that they propose are meant as playful and innovative bases for new structures. Computational methods applied to design without a fundamental understanding of human needs lead to monsters, however. Since contemporary architectural discourse has been doing exactly that — designing without having people in mind — for decades, I don't believe that we are seeing anything new; only the old alien forms are now generated by even more powerful computer programs. I sincerely hope that impressionable architecture students do not become seduced by the technological power put at their disposal, and will instead realize that power can be misused for evil purposes. One can easily lose sight of adaptive design and instead become fascinated by the technology of digital manipulation and the generation of strange forms.*

TRAINING ARCHITECTURE STUDENTS TO
ACT WITHOUT ANY CONSCIENCE

» Architecture schools teach students to create novel forms without thinking about future inhabitants
» Promote architecture as a sculptural art never meant for human occupation
» "Just a game" — oblivious of the moral responsibility for their designs

DENIAL OF HUMAN QUALITIES VALIDATED BY FAMOUS NAMES

» Famous architects manipulate forms while ignoring living beings
» Architecture schools teach students values based upon buildings as totemic objects — without humans
» Is there an innate integrity that stops young architects from mindlessly practicing an inhuman architecture?

The old system of architectural education instilled (and continues to do so at most institutions) ideological constructs as the highest values in the minds of several generations of persons, a belief system that is totally dependent upon the survival of the system in power. In other words, we have constructed a society based on an ephemeral intellectual base, destined to disappear as soon as the institutions founded on a particular power hierarchy dissolve. Such a system has no responsibility towards human society: it pays attention only to individuals internal to the logic of political favoritism.

PHILIP ZIMBARDO

» Psychologist who undertook the "Stanford Prison Experiment" — students turned into sadistic prison guards when given authority
» Similar experiment by Stanley Milgram — students administered lethal electric shocks when ordered to do so (they didn't know the current was off!)

QUESTION OF RESPONSIBILITY

» Zimbardo investigated the Abu Ghraib prison scandal (Baghdad)
» His findings — ordinary intelligent people will commit atrocities if they believe they are following authority
» Therefore, need to train students to accept responsibility for their designs!

There is no innate mechanism that will prevent an architecture student from designing an environment that is hostile to human sensibilities, so we cannot leave the student to recognize if this is happening or not. Students believe they are following authority. The present authorities (famous architects, architectural instructors) tell them that it is all right to pursue their creativity without worrying about the designed form's effect on the wellbeing of users. That is not a concern at present in architectural education. We have to reverse this process before it is too late, before those students go out and unthinkingly produce sadistic designs.

"INTELLIGENCE-BASED DESIGN"

» Trilogy by N.A.S. and Kenneth Masden
» A. "Architecture: Biological Form and Artificial Intelligence" (2006)
» B. "Restructuring 21st Century Architecture Through Human Intelligence" (2007)
» C. "Intelligence-Based Design: A Sustainable Foundation For Worldwide Architectural Education" (2008)

NEW APPROACH TO ARCHITECTURE AND EDUCATION

» Uses human intelligence to design and build the most humane environments
» Utilizes the most recent scientific knowledge about human wellbeing
» Respects level 3: the spiritual level of human beings
» Introduces opposite methods from formal and image-based design

CONCLUSION

» Teach students why a cute design on the computer screen can become a monster when actually built
» Their responsibility to learn techniques for evaluating the effects their designs will have on human beings
» **Design integrity: moral and natural — do no harm, do only good, what we build must be integral with the natural world**

LECTURE 9:
SYMMETRIES AND
THE VALUE OF ORNAMENT.

9.1. SYMMETRY PRODUCTION

HUMANS CREATE SYMMETRY

» Humans throughout history have produced multiple symmetries in artifacts, buildings, and cities
» The cultural record demonstrates an essential need for symmetry in our environment
» Not simplistic, but complex symmetry

I need to point out that most architects and urbanists understand "symmetry" to refer only to a simplistic overall symmetry, such as bilateral symmetry, but that's not what I am talking about. I am describing multiple types of symmetries on many different scales.

WHY WE NEED SYMMETRIES

» Random information is too much for human cognitive system to handle
» In a random design, every single point has to be coded for representation
» Symmetries significantly reduce the amount of information that needs to be processed by the brain

COGNITIVE ALARM

» Our neural system evolved to interpret our environment
» Random information overwhelms our cognition, thus causing alarm
» The same occurs for visually empty environments — unnatural, hence physiologically threatening

The evolutionary mechanism that created our neural/sensory system is tuned to signal alarm at identifiable threats, but also unease at situations we cannot interpret, which could hide a threat. We either understand a threatening situation through our information processing system, or feel uneasy if we do not have sufficient information to make an informed judgment. We feel at ease only in positive feedback situations that resonate with our cognition: i.e., those we can interpret positively as non-threatening.

DIFFERENT TYPES OF SYMMETRY

» Translational symmetry — shift something along one direction
» Reflectional symmetry about an axis

» Rotational symmetry about a point
» Glide reflection — combines translation with reflection

Translational symmetry

TRANSLATIONAL SYMMETRY

» Straight line defines symmetry axis
» Repetition of non-trivial units
» Alternation defines the repeating unit better, by using contrast, than simply
  empty repetition
» "Alternating repetition" (Lecture 6)

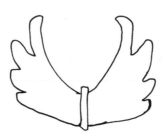

Reflectional symmetry

REFLECTIONAL SYMMETRY

» Mirror symmetry about some axis
» Any axis is fine on the floor
» But vertical axis is essential for our physiological feeling of stability
» Mirror symmetry must define an implicit vertical axis — otherwise design
  or structure feels unbalanced

A horizontal symmetry axis lying along the ground can be defined in an arbitrary direction, or by solar, planetary, or stellar alignment, such as occurred in ancient temples. The horizontal symmetry axis can also be dictated by cultural and religious considerations, as when pointing towards a specific compass direction. Any vertical symmetry axis that points up, on the other hand, is dictated by physics. Our physiology is set to the vertical axis.

IMPLICIT AXIS

» A symmetric form implicitly defines its axis of symmetry (not explicit)
» Human reaction to axis of symmetry is the same as the reaction to visible line
» Vertical or horizontal — positive
» Diagonal — negative (causes anxiety)

PHYSIOLOGICAL REACTION

» Human sensory system evolved with gravity, to orient us to gravity
» Vertical axis built into our physiology
» We react with alarm or nausea to non-vertical axes (explicit or implicit)
» Reaction cannot be learned or changed

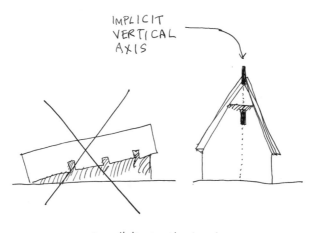

Implicit vertical axis

The vertical axis defined by gravity is not merely a visual effect, but involves the finely-tuned balance mechanisms of the inner ear. Those determine our orientation in three-dimensional space. Through a coincidence of our physiology, the inner-ear mechanism is linked to the sensation of nausea, thus dizziness from disequilibrium triggers nausea that induces vomiting, and vice-versa, food poisoning triggers vomiting that induces dizziness.

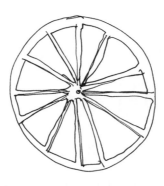

Rotational symmetry

ROTATIONAL SYMMETRY

» Great stained-glass windows in medieval cathedrals
» Open ground plans of religious buildings and circular plazas
» Rotationally invariant architectural elements are usually embedded into a larger symmetric scale

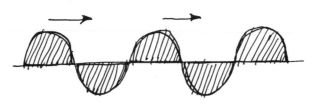

Glide reflections

GLIDE REFLECTIONS

» Combine translations with reflections into new symmetry
» There are a total of 14 ways we can combine the three fundamental symmetries nontrivially
» Glide reflections is only the first combination — there exist 13 more

THE 17 PLANE SYMMETRY GROUPS

» Combinations of the basic symmetries: translation, reflection, and rotation — used on the small scales
» Regular tiling patterns — one complex tile repeats to fill in plane
» Known as the "wallpaper groups"

SYMMETRIES OF CULTURE

» Great achievement of the human brain
» Found in all human art and artifacts
» Very sophisticated examples of the 17 plane symmetries throughout history
» But they were ERASED BY 20TH CENTURY MINIMALISM!

THE ARCH-RACIST LE CORBUSIER

» "Decoration is of a sensorial and elementary order, as is color, and is suited to simple races, peasants and savages ... The peasant loves ornament and decorates his walls."
» — Le Corbusier, "Towards a New Architecture", 1927; page 143

Unfortunately, *no one asked Le Corbusier while he was alive whether he was referring to the vast majority of human beings who use color and ornament to make their daily lives more pleasant. And what about the great religious traditions of the world, all of which identify color and ornamentation as necessary in seeking closeness to the Deity? Did Le Corbusier mean that all religious people who worship in traditionally ornamented temples are savages?*

AUTHORITY CONDEMNS SYMMETRIES

» Ideology behind dominant design system erases multiple symmetries on all the smaller scales
» Instead, it insists upon simplistic overall symmetry on the largest scale
» Our artifacts and built environment are lifeless without complex symmetries

9.2. SYMMETRY BREAKING.

PREVENTS INFORMATIONAL COLLAPSE

» It all has to do with information compression
» The human brain gains most sensory pleasure from designs that can be compressed, but not too easily
» Representation code should be neither too long (random design), nor too short

IDENTICAL REPEATED UNITS

» Contain very little information
» Just one unit repeated indefinitely
» Representation code is very short: "describe one unit, then repeat it indefinitely"

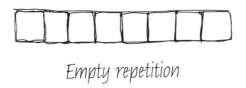

Empty repetition

JUST A LITTLE MORE INFORMATION

» Establishes larger scale by taking advantage of symmetry breaking
» Change units enough so they are no longer informationally collapsible into one identical unit
» But do not change them so much that translation or reflection symmetry is lost — then they become random

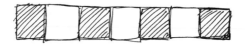

Alternating repetition (Lecture 6)

INFORMATIONAL RICHNESS

» Monotonous repetition is unsatisfying precisely because it is compressible
» The mind craves richer information
» Symmetry breaking provides variety by carefully introducing randomness on particular scales

It is not unreasonable to assume that our mind seeks informational input that corresponds to the environment in which we evolved as a species. That would be a savannah: i.e., a complex, fractal environment in which the complexity is very highly ordered into separated trees, rocks, ground, etc. This degree of ordered complexity establishes a reference for our physiology. Departures from this reference in either direction signal alarm. Disordered environments create informational overload, whereas minimalist environments create information deficit.

Symmetry breaking

TRADITIONAL ARTIFACTS

» Look carefully at traditional artifacts
» Repetition is most often NOT simple
» Repeating units always have subtle changes, on a certain scale
» Symmetry and symmetry breaking are found co-existing on distinct scales

ROUGHNESS

» Symmetries found in both nature and in human artifacts are approximate
» This is a much more sophisticated mathematical notion than regularity
» "Roughness" property (Lecture 6) breaks perfect symmetry

It would be more correct to denote "symmetry breaking" as "symmetry enhancement". The idea is to preserve the overall symmetry — which satisfies informational compression — while introducing variety. Variety has to be injected into a scale smaller than that of the larger symmetry, otherwise it will ruin the positive grouping effects of the overall symmetry. Thus, variety appears within a larger symmetry. In most cases, it is this variety that is responsible for generating smaller scales of structure, which would otherwise be missing. And it is precisely this variety that is condemned by the Modernist design canon intent upon mechanical uniformization and monotonous repetition.

Alternating repetition with symmetry breaking

SYMMETRY BREAKING CREATES IRREDUCIBLE HIERARCHY

» Symmetry breaking establishes hierarchy in a sophisticated manner
» Larger scale in a scaling hierarchy is fixed when the smaller scale can no longer be collapsed into one unit
» **Symmetry breaking stabilizes the hierarchy against collapse**

ARTISAN WORK

» We value artisanal production of the same artifact, because of the inevitable minor variations
» A wall of identical machine-made tiles is not as attractive as a wall made of imperfect hand-painted tiles
» The brain perceives the effect of minor variations in the individual tiles!

One often sees a 20C design prejudice in describing traditional artifacts: "these people did not have the technology to make perfect symmetries, so their art is rough and approximate". This statement misunderstands the sophisticated mathematical goal of symmetry breaking and roughness, which is to prevent informational collapse. Cultures certainly could create much more perfect and accurate symmetries, if they wished, but they had no desire to do so. The connoisseur and antique markets, on the other hand, certainly value artisanal production for its sophistication due to minor variations.

9.3. CLASSICAL MOLDINGS

METHOD OF SYMMETRY GENERATION

» Unexpected support from (and for) the Classical form language
» Moldings presented as the atomic units of Classical architecture
» Educational system of Donald M. Rattner (architect, New York City)

COMBINATORIAL ELEMENTS

» Moldings are the smallest elements in the Classical form language
» THEY ARE ALL SYMMETRIC
» Classical moldings are used in combination to create large-scale units
» Never taught in architecture schools!

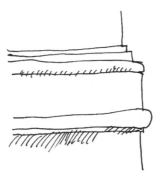

Moldings add translational symmetry

EXPRESS GRAVITATIONAL FORCE

» Moldings express the effects of gravity by appropriate horizontal articulations
» Mimic the effects of squeezing materials through weight
» Moldings are NOT decorative, but directly enhance human wellbeing
» Opposite aim from Le Corbusier's deliberate "anti-gravity" typologies

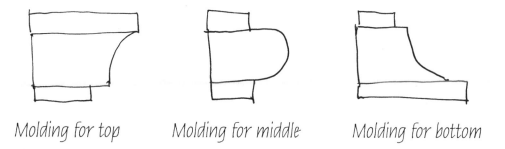

Molding for top   Molding for middle   Molding for bottom

VARIETY OF MOLDINGS

» Actually, within the three categories of moldings for top, middle, and bottom, there are further internal variations
» Classical architecture uses all of these to achieve solidity and balance
» Classical architecture also satisfies universal scaling through moldings

COMBINATORICS FOR MOLDINGS

» Language of moldings is already part of the Classical design vocabulary
» ALTERNATION, CONTRAST, SCALE, REPETITION, COORDINATION, PROPORTION, REDUCTION, etc.
» Compare with Alexander's observed 15 fundamental properties (Lecture 6)

The Classical design vocabulary already contains elements of Alexander's 15 fundamental properties. A two millennia-old design system provides a working example of the properties, as do other traditional systems of architectural design. We should not be surprised that all adaptive form languages satisfy these properties. Independent evolution converges upon similar results (in this case, form languages), precisely because of a mechanism of adaptation to both physical tectonics and human physiology.

UNIVERSALITY AND ADAPTATION

» The Classical form language is one of the most successful ever discovered
» It has evolved its own version of mathematical coherence
» This is why the Classical language has been so useful, and for so long
» It is also extremely adaptive!

WORLD ARCHITECTURE

» Every place has evolved its traditional form language (not Classical)
» During many centuries, the Classical language was applied around the world
» Buildings adapted to include elements from the local form language
» Dismissed as "hybrid" by modernists!

CLASSICAL ADAPTATIONS

» From the Greeks and Romans, to the European colonial powers, buildings have adapted to the local vernacular
» Extremely successful "colonial" buildings, now totally ignored by architectural historians
» Among the most loved older examples!

Colonial architecture gave rise to buildings in a Classical form language adapted to local climate and needs, successfully mixing with local traditional and vernacular form languages. Some colonial buildings are nowadays among the most beloved local buildings. At the same time, these buildings simply "don't exist" for modernist architectural historians. When those countries threw out occupying powers in the 20C, they inevitably accepted the modernist design vocabulary as the only politically correct expression of "independence". It was only later realized that modernist buildings are totally unsuitable to the local climate and culture, being far less adaptive than the formerly despised colonial buildings.

EMPHASIS ON THE SMALLEST SCALE

» Classical moldings are an essential component of this form language
» They help to establish the smallest scale, by focusing on it directly
» According to our theory of design coherence, the smallest scale supports all the higher-order forms

NEW APPROACH TO DESIGN

» We take Donald Rattner at his word: use moldings as atomic units of design
» Design a project by starting with the most appropriate moldings
» Then connect the moldings with plane surfaces (wall, ceiling, floor)
» Bottom-up process of design

DUALITY BETWEEN UNITS AND CONNECTIONS

» Which are the tectonic units, and which are the connections?
» Theory of centers tells us there is no distinction — we have a duality:

» A. MOLDINGS CONNECT PLANES
» B. PLANES CONNECT MOLDINGS

Duality between moldings and walls raises moldings to the same relevance as the walls themselves. Mathematically, moldings can no longer be considered as "irrelevant", whose worth depends strictly upon stylistic preferences. Moldings are just one of the essential structural elements that help to generate the hierarchy of scales necessary for coherence.

SUPPORT FROM THE FUNDAMENTAL STRUCTURE OF MATTER

» The duality between units and their connecting "glue" has a precedent
» The same phenomenon occurs in elementary particle physics
» Basic units of the physical universe
» Physics supports our theory of design!

9.4. ELEMENTARY PARTICLE SYMMETRIES

INTERNAL SYMMETRIES

» Analogy from fundamental physics
» Elementary particle interactions are symmetric under the group SU(3) (analogous to rotational invariance in a space of internal dimensions)
» But symmetry breaking also occurs in elementary particle symmetries

Architecture students and practicing architects never have to learn elementary particle physics. And yet, there are profound similarities between the microscopic structure of matter, and the large-scale structures erected by architects. I wish to make some analogies here, which shed light upon symmetry processes occurring in architectural design. A reader can try to understand this material by analogy to rotational symmetries (in some three-dimensional space) introduced at the beginning of this chapter. The main lesson is that perfect symmetry in the internal space of elementary particle properties does not allow the formation of matter as we know it! It is necessary to break perfect symmetries in order to build up the universe. This happens "spontaneously", and that's why the process is called "spontaneous symmetry breaking".

DEGENERATE NUCLEON

» With perfect hypercharge symmetry, there is only one nucleon (neutron and proton comprise the atomic nucleus)
» But that would mean no atoms!
» Spontaneously broken hypercharge symmetry creates different particles:
» N nucleon, Σ particle, Λ particle, Ξ particle, each with different mass

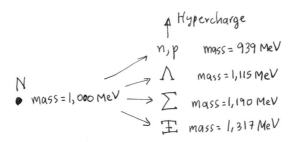

Breaking hypercharge symmetry

Let me explain what is happening. First of all, there exists an amazing symmetry (analogous to an object being rotationally invariant about some point) among the broad family of elementary particles, called N, that make up atomic nuclei. This is shown by the extremely close values for the masses of all the elementary particles shown above. Second, there are 5 experimentally observed specific families of particles instead of one, and because of this, we say that the "hypercharge" symmetry is broken. That is, there is a major and overall symmetry to begin with, but it is violated slightly, and this slight violation generates all the 5 particle families.

ELECTROMAGNETIC SYMMETRY BREAKING

» There is a further breaking of the symmetry along the isospin axis
» Creates particles with different charge
» N separates into n (neutral) and p (+)
» • Σ separates into Σ^-, Σ^0 and Σ^+
» • Ξ separates into Ξ^- and Ξ^0

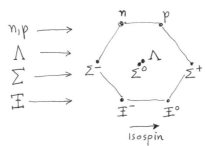

Breaking isospin symmetry

Things get more complicated because elementary particle symmetries *are described by means of an analogy to a three-dimensional space of rotations. We have seen previously that the perfect symmetry is broken in one direction (the hypercharge axis), and now we see a further and separate symmetry breaking along another, orthogonal direction (the isospin axis). Again, the overall symmetry has been violated slightly, but this violation has endowed elementary particles with different charge (either positive, neutral, or negative). Each specific particle family is observed in states with different charge. As everyone knows, charged particles will either attract or repel each other, so this second symmetry breaking has fundamental consequences for how these particles interact with one another. Indeed, this second symmetry breaking introduces electromagnetism into the universe.*

SUMMARY OF THESE RESULTS

» Fundamental constituents of matter have strong but approximate symmetry
» Small symmetry breaking is necessary to generate mass and charge
» Mass is responsible for matter!
» Charge is responsible for atoms!

To summarize, the elementary constituents of matter obey certain symmetries. Without further differentiation, however, there would be no interactions and hence no universe. Therefore, the overall large-scale symmetries of elementary particles are enhanced (broken) by smaller-scale variations, which differentiate the different particles from each other. The differentiated particles can then interact with each other to create building blocks through contrast (bound opposites) and all matter as we see around us (and which constitutes our own structure).*

ANALOGY AND IMPLICATIONS FOR DESIGN

» Strong but imperfect symmetries give rise to living structure
» Observed symmetry breaking has a remarkable parallel in broken elementary particle symmetries
» Local rotational symmetry on the small scales, imperfect on the large scale

Broken large-scale translational symmetry containing perfect small-scale rotational symmetries

LARGE-SCALE VERSUS SMALL-SCALE SYMMETRIES

» Analogy with fundamental physics
» Imperfect large-scale symmetries, but essential symmetries on the smallest scales — in internal dimensions
» Something fundamental is happening on the small scale, also in architecture and urbanism

Architecture *is an expression of natural forces, and is not a separate, purely artistic endeavor. Therefore, the laws of structure of the natural universe are highly relevant for architecture, either directly, or by analogy. Strong but imperfect large-scale symmetries order the universe. At the same time, symmetry breaking is known to be responsible for the universe itself, since without symmetry breaking in elementary particles, matter as we know it cannot exist.*

9.5. BINDING ENERGY

MASS-ENERGY RELATION

» Well-known conversion relation between mass and energy
» $E = mc^2$ (where c is the speed of light)
» Derived by Albert Einstein
» Energy is needed to bind components of mass together into larger wholes

COMBINE SUBATOMIC CONSTITUENTS

» Constituents will not bind together without extra binding energy, but will forever remain as separate units
» Binding energy is the "glue" of matter
» Mass of the whole equals mass of constituents plus the binding energy

In *both physics and architecture, if you just position components next to each other, they will not necessarily bind to create a larger, coherent whole. Proximity does not guarantee cohesion. Extra "binding energy" is necessary, otherwise all we have is a collection of disconnected units that are not really components of any system. Binding requires energy. I will review the various levels at which components of physical matter bind together to create mass. The following list goes down in scale, from the molecular level, to the atomic level, to the nuclear level, to the elementary particle level.*

SOME BASIC PHYSICAL BOUND STATES (IN DECREASING SIZE)

» Atoms bind together to form molecules
» Nuclei and electrons bind together to form atoms
» Nucleons (*n* and *p*) bind together to form the atomic nucleus
» Quarks bind together to form nucleons (neutron, proton, other octet members Λ, Σ^-, Σ^0 and Σ^+, Ξ^- and Ξ^0)

....

It is worth reminding the reader that, without symmetry breaking as discussed in the previous section, there could not be any binding at all, since that occurs only between elements with complementary characteristics. Molecules usually form from oppositely charged ions (for example, common salt binds sodium Na$^+$ with chlorine Cl$^-$); a nucleus is positively charged because it consists of protons and neutrons and binds to the negatively-charged orbital electrons to create an atom; the nucleons n ($-1/2$) and p ($+1/2$) have opposite values of isospin and consequently bind together to form the atomic nucleus; and similar considerations govern quark couplings.

....

AMOUNT OF BINDING ENERGY

» How much binding energy is required to bind a component to make a larger coherent whole?
» It depends on the size of the whole!
» As we go down in scale, the binding energy becomes as large as the mass

BINDING ENERGY AS PERCENTAGE OF THE MASS OF THE UNIT

» An electron binding to an atomic nucleus makes an atom: ratio is 5eV/0.5MeV $= 10^{-5} = 0.001\%$
» A nucleon binding to another nucleon makes an atomic nucleus: ratio is 8MeV/940MeV $= 10^{-2} = 1\%$
» A quark binding to another quark makes a nucleon: ratio is 1GeV/1GeV $= 1 = 100\%$

....

I have listed the amount of binding energy required to join a physical component into a larger whole, compared to the component's mass. Using the Einstein mass-energy relation, we can write the mass as an equivalent energy, and thus express the ratio of binding energy to the component's mass as a simple fraction. The relative binding energy increases as the size of the constituents decreases, because the binding forces become stronger on the smaller scales. Even more curious is the observation that when we get down to the smallest building blocks of matter, the quarks, the binding energy becomes as large as the mass of the quarks themselves; that is, in the limit of the smallest observable scale of fundamental matter, mass itself is indistinguishable from binding energy.

....

BINDING ENERGY IN ARCHITECTURE

» In physics, binding energy becomes matter on the lowest scale
» In architecture, the smallest perceivable scale is ornamental
» Here, the binding energy becomes the design itself
» Ornament becomes substance

If components are large (on some relative scale), the binding energy needed is small. If components are small, the binding energy needed is large. This result gives an extremely interesting analogy for architecture. I take results from subatomic physics and apply them by analogy to the macroscale. According to this thesis, large forms need a little binding energy relative to their size, whereas small architectural components require a lot of binding energy. At the limit of the smallest architectural scales, the components cannot be distinguished from the binding energy (connections) used to hold them together coherently.

ANALOGY WITH ARCHITECTURE

» Perceivable quality of substance in architecture is analogous to the mass in physical matter
» Positive substance anchors a building in our cognition, making it possible for us to connect to that structure
» Achieved by combining different tectonic components into a whole

"GLUE" BECOMES SUBSTANCE

» In architecture and urbanism, the strongest binding energy acts on the smallest perceivable scale to humans
» Tectonic components are held together in our mind by connections, symmetries, and symmetry breaking
» At the smallest scale, the binding glue itself becomes the substance!

The lesson I draw from the analogy with elementary particle physics is that important things occur on the smaller scales, and the effects get more important as we go down in scale. As the scales in a building decrease downwards, our perceptive system pays more and more immediate attention to the biological range of scales (i.e. 1 meter and below, down to the grain in the materials). Traditional architectures expressed this phenomenon by introducing ornamentation and by using natural materials in a way that generates visual and structural interest. During the twentieth century, however, this process was reversed in the search for "pure" empty forms within a minimalist design canon. I argue that architecture loses something fundamental from this negation, and that this loss goes much deeper than a simple stylistic preference.

THE NECESSITY FOR ORNAMENT

» **Binding on the smallest scale is essential for coherence and sense of substance in any building, of any shape or size**
» At the level of ornamentation, the connections become the object itself
» All larger scales are dependent upon the smallest scale — ornamentation

PRECISION IS NOT ORNAMENT!

» Modernist buildings sometimes have a precision on the smallest scale
» Precise alignment of straight edges
» But precise edges do not generate any coupling or binding energy!
» No small units; no coupling; no binding energy — form is dead

....

Precision *of design and construction is an attractive intellectual idea, but it does not generate any binding energy, hence does not contribute to the coherence of the whole. Nevertheless, the idea of precision and alignment is highly touted by modernist architects as something to strive towards. I believe that this obsession with precision obscures the need for binding energy. Arguing from another direction, binding often results in "roughness", and ornament is most often imprecise. Therefore, insisting upon precision in design may actually prevent design coherence through binding. Those very precise, intellectually pleasing buildings then have a "dead" design.*

....

ORNAMENT IS OFTEN IMPRECISE

» Ornament often requires imprecision
» "Roughness" property of Alexander
» This is not a celebration of sloppiness, but an intrinsic phenomenon
» Paying attention to the binding energy does not permit us the luxury of being concerned with useless precision

CONCLUSION: ARCHITECTURAL LIFE DEPENDS UPON ORNAMENT

» Living quality of structure and form comes from binding energy
» Ultimately depends strongly upon lowest scale — that of ornament
» Architecture = form + ornament
» Ornament becomes substance

LECTURE 10:
CODES THAT GENERATE
LIVING URBAN STRUCTURE.

10.1. GENERATIVE CODES
AND THEIR APPLICATION TO BUILDING
AND URBAN MORPHOLOGY.
10.2. SECULARIZATION DESTROYS PUBLIC SPACE.
10.3. SPIRITUAL ARCHITECTS.
10.4. LEGALIZING CODES.

10.1. GENERATIVE CODES.

URBAN GENETICS

- » Rules that tell you how to build
- » The codes evolve the form of what you build, as you are building it
- » Specify the process, not final form
- » Different from static (form-based) codes (good and bad) used today

FORM-BASED CODES

- » Form-based codes do not specify a sequence of transformations
- » Zoning ordinance specifies final form directly, but not the adaptive evolution of form
- » Form-based codes need adaptivity built in (not usually done)

TWO TYPES OF DEVELOPER CODES

- » Bad form-based codes generate inhuman forms and urban regions
- » Most of today's urban codes are bad
- » Good form-based codes can generate healthy environments
- » New Urbanist codes foster a wide range of human activity on all scales, protecting each from the others

This distinction is mathematical and biological, not ethical. A good form-based code has the potential to accommodate all sorts of different activities for a large variety of people: normal daily routines for healthy adults, pedestrian movement and play by children, an environment friendly for older, infirm, and handicapped people, etc. Good form-based codes can accommodate bicycles and slow vehicles while protecting pedestrians, etc. All of these activities have different structural needs; nevertheless they must coexist in a healthy mix. Bad codes normally ignore or eliminate altogether most uses and users other than fast-moving vehicles.

LOVE AND OWNERSHIP

- » People only care for what they love
- » Deeper ownership than simply buying a place — love cannot be bought!
- » We love something we have created
- » Therefore, people must have a hand in creating and maintaining a place

COMMUNITY COMES FROM PUBLIC SPACE

» Urban community is a consequence of a successful public space
» THERE IS NO COMMUNITY OTHERWISE
» The 20th century has no community, because modernism destroyed the built environment's public spaces

GENERATIVE CODES

» Start by intuitively sensing the possible configurations of what can be built on the land — Shinto method
» Proceed step-by-step to generate centers (in the sense of Alexander)
» Imbue land with structure that enhances and creates life there: adaptivity
» Do not destroy existing life on sites

DIFFERENT PARADIGM FOR "LIFE"

» No architect or planner talks about the "life of the site" nowadays
» Site is usually assumed to be lifeless, meant only to be cleared
» Act of building imposes human will
» We are proposing the opposite method — building to enhance the life of sites

There is a "life" in the geometry, in the configuration of the site and what exists there before building anything new. This represents a fundamental philosophical difference between our method and current practice, which is rather insensitive to the "life" of the site. Only members of our group of architects and urbanists talk about this concept. Here is a summary of the methods for implementing design that respects the "life" of the site.

"NEW URBANISM AND BEYOND"

» Two chapters in the book edited by Tigran Haas, Rizzoli, New York, 2008
» Chapter 1.1. "Generative Codes", Christopher Alexander, Randy Schmidt, Brian Hanson, Maggie Moore & Michael Mehaffy
» Chapter 10.2. "Growing Sustainable Suburbs", Lucien Steil, N.A.S. & Michael Mehaffy

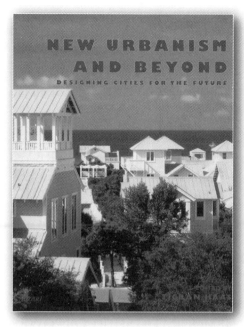

„New Urbanism and Beyond"

REVIEW OF SIX STEPS FROM "NEW URBANISM AND BEYOND"

- » 1. Any new structure must enhance existing adaptive life of the neighborhood
- » 2. Not disconnected speculative building
- » 3. Design done right on the physical site
- » 4. Layout done by consensus with users
- » 5. Using a pattern language
- » 6. Transferred to paper only after complete

PUBLIC SPACES

- » Main pedestrian spaces are chosen by consensus with users
- » Choose to save the most sacred areas by turning them into public spaces
- » Life of surrounding region is rooted in its public spaces

REVOLUTION IN DEVELOPMENT

- » Replace old paradigm where money takes absolute control of urban form
- » Concentrated power corrupts the project's design — inhuman result
- » Developer or government funding the project must share power †
- » We introduce a democratic solution

THREE-WAY SEPARATION OF POWERS

- » Copy the US constitution
- » Legislative, judicial, and executive branches of government
- » All are independent — separation guarantees democratic government
- » Safeguard against totalitarianism

THE THREE BRANCHES OF URBANISM

- » A. RULES: urbanists make up the proper rules for generating healthy urban fabric
- » B. PROJECT MANAGER: oversees the application of those rules, acting within governmental regulations
- » C. INSTITUTION: developers, builders, and architects who apply our rules to build new urban fabric and repair existing one

DEMOCRATIC SHIFT OF POWER

- » Humanistic urbanism requires a fundamental shift in power
- » The developer/financier or government will NOT control entire process
- » Power belongs with the current or future residents, and is exercised though their chosen project manager

PROJECT MANAGER

- » Project manager has to be legally independent of profit motive
- » Cannot be influenced by developer
- » Works for (and is paid by) the community, not the builder
- » Receives a fixed fee, no kickbacks
- » Maintains human quality of project

PROJECT MANAGER (CONT.)

- » Has some direct control of subcontractors (who are working not strictly through overall contractor)
- » Directs craftsmen to be more autonomous in their designs
- » Supervises periodic adjustment of design to allow for spontaneity

NEW BUSINESS PLAN

- » Developer finances and profits from the project (and can make even more profit using our three-way model)
- » BUT DOES NOT HAVE CONTROL OF THE DESIGN PROCESS
- » That is the primary responsibility of the independent project manager

NEW BUSINESS PLAN (CONT.)

» New type of agreement signed between owner and architect
» Protect autonomy from legal liability
» Different type of contract, addendum to permit craftsmen to have expression
» Allows craftsmen to be involved in the process of design while building

It is extremely easy to get a contract addendum approved by the American Institute of Architects, and simply attach it to the overall contract. Thus, the legal issues concerning the new business plans are easily solved under the present operational framework. It is neither necessary nor desirable to prepare a contract that specifies everything in minute detail so that nothing is flexible. There is no room for creativity under the present type of contract. The idea of a new business plan was developed by Christopher Alexander and applied in many of his projects (see his recent books for details). It allowed a flexibility to create the best parts of the project by the redistribution of funds, which would have been impossible otherwise.

QUALITY CONTROL

» Project manager supervises craftsmen and holds periodic design reviews
» Control of quality through eyes on site, not by legal reference to paper design
» New type of contract protects all parties from litigation over innovation

GRAMEEN MODEL FOR REPAIR

» Finance system for individual repairs modeled on the Grameen Bank
» Small loans to home-owners to undertake their own repairs
» NOT CONTROLLED BY DEVELOPER
» New code forbids profit from change orders (used to stop adaptation in buildings)

BOTTOM-UP BALANCE

Small-scale funding introduces a bottom-up component of development to balance the usual top-down process
Actually, this is the standard model in most of the developing world today
Only smaller funding distribution can develop living urban spaces

COMMUNITY BUDGET

» Budget delegated to build and maintain public space (as used in gated communities)
» Outdoor walls, gardens, seats, paths, trees, fountains, maintained by community budget
» Drastically different from procurement process driving suburban sprawl today

IN NON-SPECULATIVE APPLICATION

» One approach: land owners finance their project, and hire a project manager to facilitate design
» Local government oversight checks that our urban rules are correctly applied to generate living geometry
» REWRITE CURRENT ZONING!

A project manager that can help to create a project with the required human qualities needs to be trained in our techniques, and to be familiar with the material that I have mentioned here. The three-way separation of powers introduced above must be strictly implemented in planning and building the project. There are distinct cases of development that follow slightly different rules, which are discussed below.

HOW DOES A DEVELOPER OR GOVERNMENT BUILD SPECULATIVELY?

» Inevitable business model for today must also meet our three-way model
» Different cases require separate powers
» A. Developer works with project manager appointed by government
» B. Government must work with local NGO-appointed project manager

FINALLY GET THE GEOMETRY RIGHT!

» For one century, we have been building according to an inhuman geometry
» Blindly following the same anti-urban typologies year after year
» Wasting land and materials to create an unloved world fit only for cars

OUR BELOVED SUBURBS ARE INHUMAN

» People buy into the utopian dream
» But suburban sprawl represents a toxic disconnectedness
» Isolated houses without community
» Useless front lawns and back yards
» Wrong geometry that "looks nice"

STOP MASSIVE LAND CLEARANCE

» Great deception: "suburbia celebrates nature" — no, it violates nature
» Nihilistic destruction of landscape
» Replaces nature with dead typologies
» Driven by the basest profit motive and by false images of utopian modernity
» We can make a profit, but not while killing the city or the land!

Present-day practice clears the land of native vegetation, especially in desert regions, and replaces it with lawn copied from romantic images of Scotland. It does look nice, in theory. We then waste valuable water resources to maintain all this lawn green, yet people hardly ever use the lawn for anything. Suburbia chases after an elusive image, but the reality is unsustainable. And this occurs at a time when drastic water shortages loom in the future, but reality is evidently not enough to change the images of utopian modernity reproducing like a virus.

REGENERATING SUBURBS

» "Growing Sustainable Suburbs", Lucien Steil, N.A.S. & Michael Mehaffy, in: "New Urbanism and Beyond"
» Need massive reconstruction effort — comparable to post-war rebuilding
» Vast regions of unsustainable sprawl
» Either regenerate or abandon them!

FIVE STEPS FOR REGENERATION

» 1. Partition into pedestrian catchment regions; semi-permeable boundaries
» 2. Increase density towards centers
» 3. Create mixed-use urban centers
» 4. Mixed-use intermediate ring
» 5. Re-configure road structure for optimum pedestrian connectivity

SOME PRACTICAL IDEAS

» Abandon currently used but inhuman process of industrial development
» Adopt new guidelines for adaptive design and construction
» Among the new ideas for practical implementation is the step-by-step decision sequence

EFFICIENCY STRATEGY USES PARETO'S 20/80 RULE

» 20% of problems take up 80% of the time and effort
» Applied to a single complex process
» Bottlenecks in 20% or less of an algorithm cause 80% or more of the overall delays
» Focus on bottlenecks, one at a time

PREPARE FOR DRASTIC CHANGE

» Not necessary to run out of petroleum
» Brazil, China, and India will take most of it to maintain their oil-dependent industry and urbanization
» We need to survive an era without oil
» Only sustainable urban reconfiguration will prevent a third world war over oil

"CONNECTING THE FRACTAL CITY"

» Chapter 6 of my book "Principles of Urban Structure", Techne Press, Amsterdam, 2005.
» Lays out theoretical framework of generating the form of living cities
» But today (in 2008) it is impossible to implement with existing zoning laws!

CODES USED TO CREATE LIFE

» DNA is coded information for all biological structure
» Creates life through genetic codes
» Same process as with urban codes
» Developing embryo uses both DNA information, and the existing geometry of the configuration at each step

DEVELOPMENT OF URBAN FORM

» Need a good set of codes
» Replace present modernist codes on the books with New Urbanist codes
» Further enhance design process by implementing generative codes
» Formation of healthy urban fabric will then occur naturally over time

MODERNIST URBANISM GROWS INHUMAN FORMS

» Building setbacks
» Monofunctional zoning
» Separation of work from residence
» Monstrous grid street patterns
» Priority given to car geometry
» Industrial construction materials

MODERNIST URBANISM (CONT.)

» Impermeable sheer walls at street level — fundamentally hostile
» No place for pedestrian
» No shared urban space

» Garages for storing consumer junk
» Residential street as parking lot

The picture in a brochure selling model houses in a new suburban development is totally misleading. Lots of green lawn with children playing on the street looks pretty, but it is a deception. When all the garages of sprawl houses become filled with junk and boxes, cars park on the driveway and on the street. No more openness, just an ugly parking lot. Then, since the suburban street is built to the width of a highway, no child is safe on the street. Even though those streets are empty most of the day, you never know when someone will speed past and kill a child. The signs stating the speed limit are next to useless. Speed bumps all over are an admission that street design has failed, and the bumps have been added as a desperate measure after the fact. They only annoy drivers.

EVEN MINIMAL "GOOD" CODES CAN MAKE AN ENORMOUS DIFFERENCE

» Begin today by implementing some sane urban codes
» For example, David Sucher's three rules for dense urban fabric
» Will solve many mistakes overnight
» Then, we can proceed with the major urban reconstruction proposed by us

DAVID SUCHER'S THREE RULES FOR CENTRAL URBAN REGIONS

» 1. Build to sidewalk (property line)
» 2. Make building front permeable
» 3. Prohibit parking lots in front of the building (only on-street parking)
» From David Sucher's book: "City Comforts", Seattle, Washington, 2003

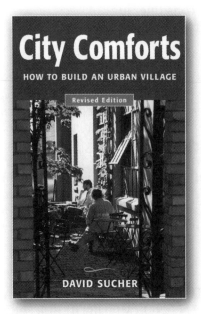

„City Comforts"

CODES THAT BUILD LIVING FABRIC

» Generative codes, combined with patterns from "A Pattern Language" cre-
ate living urban fabric
» For example, Pattern 167: "SIX-FOOT BALCONY" — (2-meters deep)
» Would improve the lives of hundreds of millions of people around the world!

10.2. SECULARIZATION DESTROYS PUBLIC SPACE.

GEOMETRY CREATES SOCIETY

» Urban space is common space
» Main function of a city
» Place of interaction between people
» Historically, public space always had a sacred quality
» Humanity relied on this space of interactions

SACRED SPACES

» Spaces that are valued by the society
» Common spaces that people are willing to defend and maintain

- » Sacred character of place
- » Sometimes, entryway to sacred ground
- » The "glue" that binds people to a place

SACRED SPACES (CONT.)

- » Oftentimes very modest
- » Can be private or public (shared)
- » Are redefined according to our secular philosophy
- » Where they do exist, we are not supposed to see them!

SACRED SPACES (CONT.)

- » Building community has to reverse the loss of spiritual values and human qualities from our society
- » "Favelas and Social Housing: the Urbanism of Self-Organization", by N.A.S., David Brain, Andrés Duany, Michael Mehaffy & Ernesto Philibert-Petit, published in a separate book

Very few places we build today have the qualities of a sacred space. In those few successful cases, the result arises through a personal vision of the individual who designs or builds them, since there is little guidance from prevailing architectural culture. We are at a loss to understand how they move us! Christopher Alexander has spelled out the prerequisite for creating sacred spaces: utter selflessness on the part of the designer while designing the space, reaching instead for qualities inherent in the space itself rather than imposing the designer's own will. Even contemporary churches — especially contemporary churches — fail to create sacred space because most of them are image-driven.

MODERNISM ERASED SACRED SPACES

- » Modernist architects turned with a vicious hatred against sacred spaces
- » Their anti-religious credo: "There is no such thing as a sacred space!"
- » Goes hand-in-hand with modernist replacement of religion with its own image-based dogma

Many churches have been built in the modernist idiom, so it might sound contradictory to condemn modernist architects for being anti-religious. Nevertheless, early modernism did arise out of and tried to incorporate socialist dogma, which was fashionable at the time. Its ideology was just as uncompromisingly hostile towards traditional religion as it was towards traditional architecture. Nowadays, decades later, there is a debate going on about the spiritual qualities of those modernist churches, and of their more recent post-modernist and deconstructivist derivatives. I personally feel that, with only a few exceptions, the religious building tradition was lost when architects embraced modernism. Most contemporary churches are not places where an individual can connect with God.

SPACES THAT REPEL HUMANS

» An urban geometry reinforced by structures that prohibit connection to the transcendental
» Fanatical insistence of machine, i.e. non-human aesthetic
» Geometry has no shared meaning
» Alien imposition on the environment

SACRED SPACES TODAY?

» We have few sacred spaces today
» Therefore, there is no "glue" to hold the contemporary city together
» Guaranteed absence by our planning codes, legislated deliberately
» They would be illegal to build now
» Have to fight against inhuman zoning

WE HAVE FORGOTTEN...

» All settlements in the past several millennia, were held together with sacred spaces
» Even in favelas today, there exist spontaneously created sacred spaces
» Minor or major urban spaces that are valued by nearby inhabitants

10.3. SPIRITUAL ARCHITECTS

REDISCOVERING THE SACRED

» Many traditional architects continue to use timeless methods of building
» Ignored by the media and academia
» Some architects in the West have re-invented these methods
» Outgrowth of "new-age" spiritual movement of the past few decades

SPIRITUAL WESTERN ARCHITECTURE

» Examples: Tom Bender (U.S.A.), Christopher Day (Britain), and many others around the world
» Their architecture is highly sensitive

- » Those architects work on connectivity with human beings and the universe
- » Successfully create life in buildings

PHENOMENOLOGY

- » Effects are perceived by human senses
- » These architects are responding to REAL forces in the environment
- » Since we don't know how to fully explain the connective process of design, it remains mystical

PREMATURE EXPLANATIONS

- » When we don't understand the mechanisms for something we observe, we usually invent a mythology for it
- » To the scientific world, this makes the phenomenon itself doubtful
- » But sometimes it takes centuries to gain a better understanding

CONSENSUS DESIGN: SOCIALLY INCLUSIVE PROCESSES

- » Christopher Day practices architecture that connects us to the sacred
- » He describes his process in: "Consensus Design", Architectural Press, Oxford, '03
- » Same process as our model uses to connect with the transcendental realm

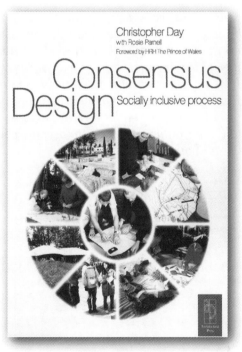

„Consensus Design"

DESIGN GROWS OUT OF SITE

» Walk around with users to perceive positioning of forms and paths
» Sensitive to nature and site's geometry
» Trace plan on paper, then build clay or plasticine model of forms on top
» Use human feelings to judge form and adjust to find optimal possibilities

CONDITIONS FOR CONNECTING

» An important lesson from spiritual architects, especially for scientists!
» Human qualities help in connecting to a higher state of being, better urbanism
» Killed by industrialization and the blind worship of the machine culture

The connection to the sacred through ordered structure and patterns was treated earlier in these lectures (see Section 4.3). I can now claim that by deliberately avoiding such mathematical connections, new religious buildings block any connection to the sacred, which is surely ironic and contradicts the essential purpose of the building. Nevertheless, organized religions have unfortunately become victims of architectural propaganda, and, being terrified of being perceived as "old-fashioned" (hence risking alienating the public), they adopt whatever fashionable architecture is promoted by the media. As a result, some of the most anti-spiritual buildings today are contemporary places of worship designed by "name" architects. It would not be too unkind to propose that those architects were inspired by the built representation of evil; and indeed, there is a striking resemblance between contemporary Christian Churches and Holocaust Museums. Some well-meaning commentators argue that a contemporary church absolutely has to interact with its congregation in the same way that those people interact with glass-and-steel skyscrapers, otherwise there is some kind of philosophical incongruence. Well, we know from neuroaesthetics that people simply do not interact with glass-and-steel skyscrapers, which cause them alienation and alarm. Critics who hold such opinions simply do not grasp that the purpose of a Church is to offer a refuge against the inhumanity of the contemporary built environment, and not to become complicit in the desacralization of our cities and our society.

10.4. LEGALIZING CODES.

A PLANNING COUP D'ÉTAT

» After the Second World War, modernist urbanists quietly took control of the planning profession
» They changed the urban codes to guarantee that all cities evolved towards modernist typologies
» Tremendous victory for urbanicides

PLANNING CODES

» Were written by lawyers into law after the Second World War
» Now those laws tie the hands of adaptive architects and urbanists
» Illegal to build humanistic structures
» No way for urbanists to change the codes, because of the state apparatus

INHUMAN URBAN CODES

» Killed the pedestrian street
» Made it illegal to mix urban functions
» Inhuman zoning is not reformable
» Will have to be ignored (which is illegal), or be totally rewritten to build or rebuild human environments

....

James *Howard Kunstler believes that our suburban sprawl is unsustainable, and will have to be abandoned with the end of cheap oil. In his nightmare scenario of societal breakdown, there is no more state structure capable of maintaining law and order, let alone enforcing these stupid urban codes. Do we have to come to that point to substitute the codes on the books today with city-regenerating codes? Illegal or not, people will eventually have to abandon those codes and replace them with New Urbanist codes.*

....

1933 — A FATEFUL YEAR

» Le Corbusier largely wrote the "1933 Charter of Athens" on board the ship "Patris" cruising the Mediterranean from Marseilles to Athens
» Codified antisocial hatred of traditional city life into a set of geometric rules
» Implemented by many governments

"THE NEW CHARTER OF ATHENS"

» Recently, a group of my friends has written a new Charter of Athens
» — European Council of Town Planners, 2003
» Proposes a sustainable network urbanism oriented towards human-scale activities and wellbeing

MODERNIST ZONING

» Modernist planners were invited to take over the world's urbanism
» Governments and corporations all swallowed the deception of "progress"
» Turned control of building over to a bunch of dangerous urbanicides
» Those, in turn, imposed their ideology

MODERNIST TAKEOVER

» When the modernists came to power they re-wrote all the planning laws
» They solidified their power by using the established legal system
» First priority of anti-humanist zoning laws was Le Corbusier's hysterical call to "kill the street!" (Lecture 8)

Modernist architects and planners commandeered the legal system to express their own narrow ideology. We need to change our planning laws. Architects and urbanists cannot achieve this: it has to be legislated. Every government has to replace their planning codes, and to do this as soon as possible. Andrés Duany offers his solution, the Smart Code (a form-based New Urbanist code) free on the internet. Christopher Alexander's results are available in his books. Our codes do not impose a form, they establish a process, which produces practical results that are uniquely adapted for each location.

CONCLUSION

» Urbanicides solidified their takeover of urbanism by co-opting the legal system
» Since then, no real change is possible
» We continue to reproduce inhuman urban typologies, because in most places today IT IS ILLEGAL TO DO OTHERWISE

LECTURE 11:
NEW URBANISM AND TALL BUILDINGS.

11.1. DUANY-PLATER-ZYBERK (DPZ) CODES.

11.2. THE NEW URBANISM.

11.3. STEPHEN MOUZON'S PROJECT.

11.4. TALL BUILDINGS.

11.1. DUANY-PLATER-ZYBERK (DPZ) CODES.

MICHAEL W. MEHAFFY

» In this lecture, I'm happy to welcome the participation of Michael Mehaffy, urbanist, philosopher, and educator
» Past Director of Education for the Prince's Foundation, London
» One of Alexander's generals: Lysimachos, Antigonos, Seleukos, Ptolemy, Mehaffy, Salingaros, *et. al.*

INTRODUCTION (MICHAEL)

» New Urbanism is about:
» The space between buildings
» The arrangement of buildings in space
» The complex connective system of public and private realms (including buildings!)

INTRODUCTION (CONT.)

» Challenges:
» The connective system of public and private realms is surprisingly complex!
» Rapid new urbanization & growth — 50% of humanity now in cities
» Environmental pressures — climate change, resource depletion, etc.

INTRODUCTION (CONT.)

» Solutions:
» Much greater urban efficiency
» Much greater urban connectivity — ability to move efficiently in many modes
» Self-organized patterns and pattern-generating tools — codes generate sustainable urban morphology

CODES THAT CREATE SOCIETY

» A practical advance in urbanism
» Form-based codes unlike the ones legally binding all urban development
» DPZ smart code enables organic, human-scale urban fabric to emerge
» But must be calibrated to local and historical sense of place

MODERNIST VERSUS NEW URBANIST

» Monoculture versus "Mixed use"
» Disconnected versus "Connected"
» Emphasis on largest scale versus "Balanced scales"
» No pedestrians versus "Protect pedestrian"
» Streets that divide versus "Streets that unify"

REPLACE ALL THE FORM-BASED CODES

» Code books are modernist
» They automatically produce a modernist car-dependent city
» They destroy the pedestrian human-oriented and human-scaled city
» The only way to reverse urban destruction is to adopt codes for traditional urbanism

"SMART CODE"

» A generic urban code that guarantees human-scale habitat
» Contains many pieces that have to be calibrated for local needs
» Does not force the same rigid typology everywhere
» Available free online from Duany-Plater-Zyberk (dpz.com)

CALIBRATION

» Measure the most wonderful examples from existing urban regions
» Different typologies for different uses
» Write measurements into code
» Adapts to locality and different uses

Calibration involves driving and walking around a city to document dimensions and measurements for the different regions of urban density. These measurements then become the basis for new building and urban re-generation. One needs to identify the best examples from the past and the present to get those measurements (for example, curbs, houses, multi-storey buildings, setbacks, trees, etc. that have not yet been destroyed). This is the urban DNA that is capable of regenerating a city. In some cases, all the DNA in a city has been corrupted, so we need to measure some other city's buildings and dimensions, therefore a "sister" city has to be identified for this task.

TRANSFERABILITY

» Smart code is written in a legal manner, so that it can replace current codes
» Switch is a purely legal matter
» Very easy to do through legislation

ANDRÉS DUANY'S FRUSTRATION

» Many prospective clients ask Andrés to do a project, but neglect to change their codes
» Impossible to build human-scale environment with the existing codes
» In most cases, you need to go outside city limits, where the government can relax the codes

11.2. THE NEW URBANISM.

A MARKET-DRIVEN REFORM

» In 1993, six urbanist firms got together to write the "Charter for the New Urbanism"
» Defined rules and practices for recovering the best of traditional urbanism in today's projects
» Did not come from academia!

Léon Krier's pie

MICHAEL MEHAFFY: NEW URBANISM'S PROMISES

» The return of urbanism is the return of the civic realm
» The return of urbanism is the return of the street
» The human patterns come first, and then the visual ideas follow — otherwise we are simply making people live in disconnected sculptures

EXPLOSIVE GROWTH

» Since the initial Congress (CNU), many firms have designed neo-traditional communities
» Some are more adaptive than others
» But new urbanist projects are getting better all the time!

Market *forces are pushing developers to create New Urbanist communities: not because of any philosophical reason, but driven by the profit motive. It's very simple. More human-scaled communities give a higher return on investment. Some builders who have created the most inhuman suburban sprawl have suddenly switched to the New Urbanist model, attracted by the economics of commercial value. Maybe they do not get perfect results, but it doesn't matter, since this is a tremendous leap towards the right direction. For this reason, we have hope for optimism. As more people get involved, competition among New Urbanist developers pushes for a higher quality product.*

DEFINES THE STREET

» Zone density in New Urbanism changes in the middle of a block, not in the middle of a road
» Therefore, street on opposite sides has the same urban character
» Street is the entity, not city block

This *is an important feature of the New Urbanism: creating the low to medium traffic street as the basic urban entity, which extends into and interconnects all the public spaces. Taking two parallel long blocks with the street between them, the buildings must cooperate in height, style, and character on either side of the enclosed street, but may change where they face another street. Building the street as a coherent whole represents a fundamental reversal from considering the "block" as an urban entity, because it just isn't experienced that way. Since density, lot size, and building height obviously must vary continuously within an urban context, and to do this along the street ruins its coherence, then such urban changes should occur across the lengthwise mid-point of the block.*

11.3. STEPHEN MOUZON'S PROJECT.

A SUCCESS TO LEARN FROM

- » Schooner Bay, Bahamas, a DPZ/New Urban Guild project
- » Stephen A. Mouzon, architect and urbanist, Miami Beach, Florida
- » Application of codes to project
- » One step at a time — Alexander

MOUZON'S METHOD

- » *"Once the paths were set, I began designing just one building at a time, not thinking about anything that would come afterwards. I worked with no intent of artistry at all … just doing the little things that made the most sense for the site in question. Only after I had completed the block did I go back to draw the lot lines on another drawing."*

MOUZON'S METHOD (CONT.)

- » *"The character of the lots could not possibly have been designed without knowing what the buildings were, I don't believe. This … is a technique we should have in the toolbox if you're looking for an organic or medieval character for a place: design first, lot lines later."*

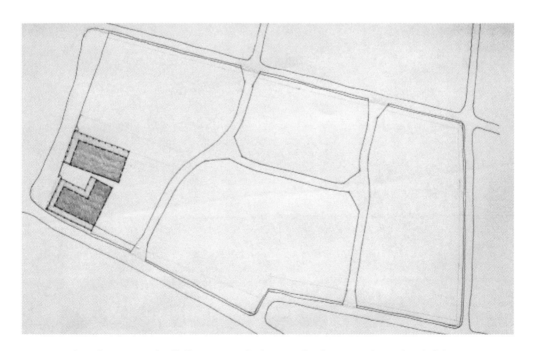

The first two buildings, and the main internal paths laid out

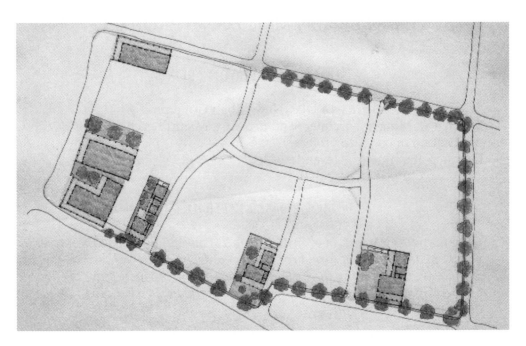

Tiny turning radii, so fix the internal chamfers

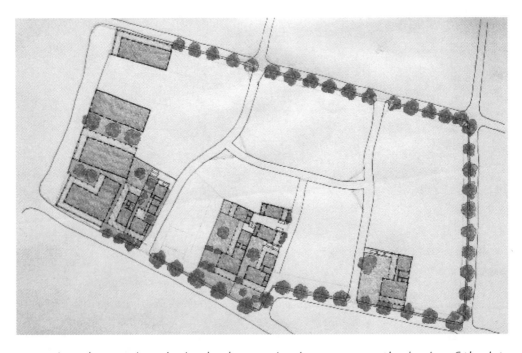

Secondary internal paths beginning to develop to access the backs of the lots

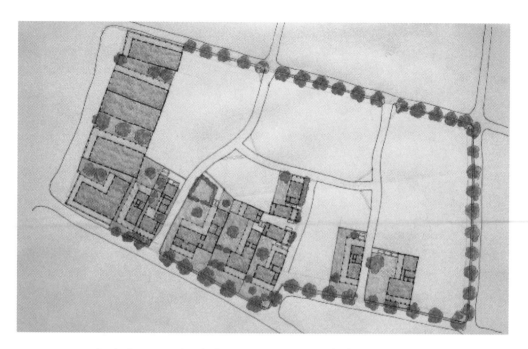

Block face to the left, now complete, is in the T5 zone

The T5 zone in the New Urbanist classification represents a downtown density, consisting of multi-storey buildings, denser than what occurs here on the right-hand-side. In this particular project, the number of storeys is still small. As mentioned earlier in this lecture, the height, density, and character of buildings (which define different T-zones) change somewhere in the middle of the block so as to guarantee that the street is an urban entity defined by a single T-zone. The street is part of urban space that creates urbanism and community. Zoning changes should be implemented where they cannot be seen. What happens in the middle of the block is of minor importance to the human perception of a city.

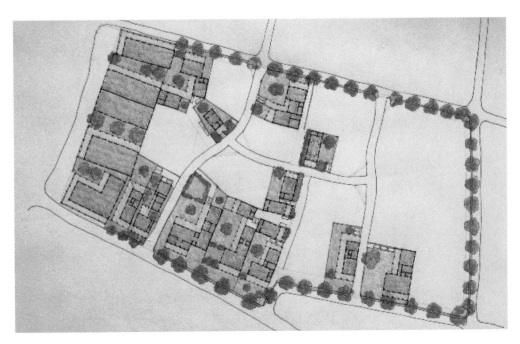

After house on the top street was designed, the location for the path became obvious

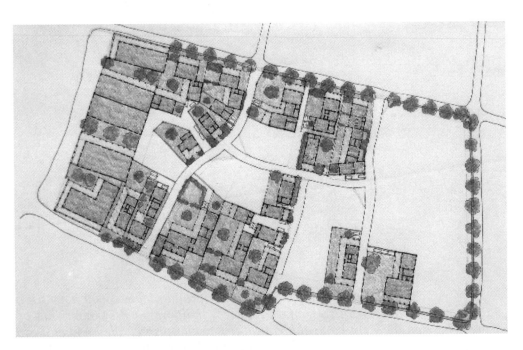

First work unit added: an office attached to the house. Actually, a number of things were added here, and Stephen Mouzon has not explicitly labeled what is intended to be work space. The crucial point is that the whole complex is intended from the very beginning to be mixed-use, so new additions may introduce new uses. It is only a coincidence of this particular project that the first buildings were residential, and subsequent additions begin to introduce other uses.

Second and third work spaces added: a shop and an office

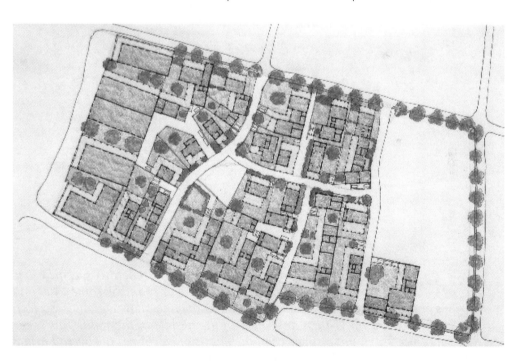

The nearly 30-foot space saved by not having cars in paths has ENORMOUS implications. Interior paths are for pedestrians, golf carts, and emergency vehicles only, and we have estimated the increased space required to build standard-size roads in their place (sure, this cannot be done everywhere)

The special conditions of this project allow cars to be kept to the periphery, which clearly cannot be applied everywhere. Stephen Mouzon
explains: "The section of Schooner Bay closest to the harbour (2-3 blocks out) is
for golf carts only, like Dunmore Town on Harbour Island. For those residents,
there is a parking lot on the edge of town, similar to many European towns. The
streets themselves are large enough for construction vehicles (one-way) but residents will either walk or ride golf carts. Sick or old people could also be brought
in via automobiles, as will deliveries to the Inn & the shops, but the idea is to
have predominantly golf cart of pedestrian traffic by all who can do so."

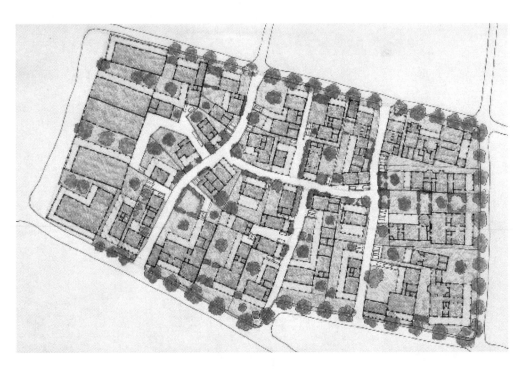

All the internal paths in this block are alleys for
pedestrians, golf carts, and emergency vehicles only

New Urbanist projects come up against overly generous specifications
insisted upon by emergency vehicles. For example, some cities and
regions oblige any suburban road to be wide enough to allow a giant American
fire engine to make a U-turn anywhere in the middle of the road. This is certainly not necessary, but a single code such as this determines the overall urban
morphology of suburbs throughout the USA. We, instead, recommend ACCESS
for emergency vehicles to every single point in the urban fabric, but this is not
the same as having all our local streets built to the specification and width of
highways. At this time, we are stuck with legal codes that need to be changed.

THANKS!

» Unpublished diagrams from the Schooner Bay project kindly provided by Stephen Mouzon
» Thanks also to DPZ and the New Urban Guild for permission to use them in this lecture

11.4. TALL BUILDINGS.

SIMPLISTIC TYPOLOGY

» Skyscrapers are usually designed according to a template
» Ignore context and environment
» Imposition of architect's will
» Can never arise from step-by-step adaptation

UNSUSTAINABLE

» Skyscrapers can never be made sustainable
» Using the latest technology does not alter their intrusive character
» They introduce urban singularity

....

While multi-use high-rise buildings go one step towards adapting tall buildings into an urban environment, modernist zoning laws forbid mixed use in many locations today. The other adaptive feature is to have a rather wide, geometrically complex, and mixed-use base that provides a human-scaled urban environment. This, however, is almost always ruled out by the modernist conceit that insists upon having a freestanding tower isolated from the urban fabric, existing purely in its own space. The ideology of the tower's "pure" form takes precedence over any possible adaptation into the city. An example of skyscrapers that work more successfully in an urban setting through their complex base is found in the Azrieli Towers in Tel-Aviv, Israel, which rise out of a large shopping mall.

....

MICHAEL MEHAFFY ON SKYSCRAPERS

» Claim that tall buildings are sustainable is a cruel fraud
» Excessive heat gain and loss from unshaded exposures and typical glazing systems
» "Heat island" effects
» Require materials with very high embedded energy

The production of high-tech materials used for glazing and "green fixes" of skyscrapers is extraordinarily expensive. Strong materials required for building skyscrapers are not cheap to produce. The energy required to produce all the very high-strength steel pollutes: the energy required to transport the steel to the site pollutes. Is the steel produced locally? No. It is probably imported from China, which has to deal with its pollution problems over there. These very energy-intensive materials appear "cleanly" on the worksite, which is deceptive. But when optimistic calculations are done by spokespersons for skyscrapers, they neglect those energy losses from the equation.

MICHAEL ON SKYSCRAPERS (CONT.)

» Skyscraper floorplates are inefficient — excessive space requirements for lifts and for emergency exit stairs
» They block sun and view
» Create wind effects at the ground level
» Carbon benefits of urban density level off at 4 to 6 storey building envelope

SOCIAL PROBLEMS

» Ground floor usually disconnected
» Alexander's Pattern 21: children living more than 4 storeys from the ground feel disconnected
» Léon Krier proposes tall buildings that are monuments, not residences

BAD TALL BUILDINGS

» Iconic monsters isolated from city
» Totems for worshipping some lousy architect's ego
» Built to be visually recognized
» "Look at me!" — an expression of kitsch sitting in a dead plaza

Since this book is about algorithmic design, it is worth pointing out that modernist skyscrapers are not the result of any computation: they are simply vertical repeats. Therefore, they represent the antithesis of design as computation, even in the abstract sense. Le Corbusier's simplistic idea "the plan is the generator" finds here its most banal and destructive expression. The negative psychological effect of floors repeating upwards monotonously comes from combinatorial complexity in the vertical direction (see Section 1.5), and contributes to the perception of the (modernist) skyscraper city as an alien, inhuman environment. Architects who collaborate with big money interests to build modernist skyscrapers are guilty of complicity in a ruthless power play, and it is surprising when they are praised for being "original" instead of being condemned. A measure of how completely the media manipulates the public mind is that such an *obviously unoriginal product can be praised worldwide as being original, and its authors awarded prestigious architectural prizes. An explanation comes not from within architecture, but from the philosopher Roger Scruton: "In this society there is only power, and the goal of power is power... Truth is what power decides, and reality [is] no more than a construct of power... Language has been turned against itself, so that the attempt to mean something will always fail." — A Political Philosophy, Continuum Press, London, 2006, page 183.*

RELIGIOUS ICONS

» Le Corbusier's "towers in the park" has become a religious symbol
» Worshipped by modernist urbanists
» Despite repeated disasters, still used as "modern" typology the world over
» … with towers of ever increasing height! People never learn…

There is something suspicious about people who never learn, in this case the large group of persons (architects, architecture critics, politicians) who continue to support the "towers in the park" idea. This is a sociological phenomenon. A person ignores physical reality usually because he/she has a religious faith in the concept. Only a religious attachment cannot be changed in the evidence of reality, of hard facts from failed experiments. But the faith is kept, and the faith is transmitted in our architecture schools. I'm not talking here of a genuine religious concept connecting to a higher order in the universe, but instead of a pseudo-religion, a genuine idolatry that worships architectural icons. Le Corbusier's diagram has a diabolical seductiveness.

GOOD TALL BUILDINGS

» Must be very few in any city
» Always in the high-density center
» Ground floor helps urban fabric
» Examples from late 19C, early 20C
» Thin, not too tall, hierarchy of scales
» No setbacks

The question of setbacks has been addressed before: a freestanding iconic building removes itself from the urban fabric and thus damages the pedestrian city. Unfortunately, we have inherited this seductive image from modernist ideology. The widely-accepted but nonetheless phony image of an adjoining "plaza" somehow humanizing a skyscraper is simply propaganda. Setbacks were a gimmick used to increase the number of floors by using a legal loophole in New York City's building codes. It's best not to experience a skyscraper up close. To function properly, an urban space needs to be partially enclosed by human-scaled building fabric, and that means permeable façades of 3-4 storey buildings (as found in traditional 19C urban fabric), not a skyscraper rising on one side.

CONCLUSION

» There are several branches of New Urbanism practiced today
» All of them are far better than zoned car-dependent sprawl, or skyscrapers in the park — a monstrous idea
» Communities the world over are building neo-traditional developments

LECTURE 12:
CHILDREN, SOCIAL HOUSING,
AND COMPUTING THE CITY.

12.1. GENERATIVE CODES
AND URBAN COMPUTATIONS.

12.2. URBAN PLAZAS.

12.3. DESIGNING FOR CHILDREN.

12.4. FAVELAS AND SOCIAL HOUSING.

12.1. GENERATIVE CODES AND URBAN COMPUTATIONS.

CODES WITH FEEDBACK

»   Generative codes depend at each stage upon the entire configuration
»   Generative codes are dynamic and recursive — the result of each step feeds into the next step
»   … unlike iterative static codes (where the same step is repeated)

A *"generative" code is an algorithm that generates a form by repeated application (Christopher Alexander). It is termed generative because it uses feedback from the form as it exists at each stage. This type of code is distinct from "static" codes that contain fixed rules, and which are applied regardless of the intermediate states of the result. Generative codes give one the opportunity to adapt the result to many different factors at hand, by adapting the code itself to the situation during computation.*

DESIGN AS COMPUTATION

»   Coherent and sophisticated structure grows, like computing a result
»   Follows from many simple steps
»   Each step is a computation
»   Altogether, we develop a recursive sequence of transformations

WHAT DOES URBANISM COMPUTE?

»   Position of buildings on the ground
»   Footprint of the buildings
»   Position of infrastructure that supplies and connects all the buildings: roads, sewerage lines, electricity grid, etc.

Monotonous repetition has been adopted as the basic paradigm of the industrial age and is not limited to the elements of urban form. Nevertheless, that approach contradicts biological algorithms (which are interactive and never simplistic) and we certainly feel this mismatch as alienation and disconnection from monotonous industrial environments. As explained in Section 1.5, the human mind seeks to understand its environment through scaling, complex symmetries, and groupings. Our cognitive system is frustrated when faced with repeating modules, which results in distress and a loss of situatedness. Since situatedness is one of the key properties of living structure, its loss (or, in the case of simplistic urbanism, its deliberate suppression) reduces the life-enhancing qualities of the built environment.

ARCHITECTURAL ALGORITHMS

» Generative codes evolve structure to satisfy human needs
» Algorithms generate complex structures on the large scale
» Final design can appear "unexpected"
» If the process is adaptive, then the large scale is relevant and correct

The question of "unexpected" form comes from the fact that the result has evolved. To allow a complex design the freedom to truly evolve, the designer must not impose any pre-conceived images, and thus the final result should possess spontaneous features that arise from the computational process itself. If, on the other hand, one begins and ends with a fixed image, then the design cannot possibly evolve to adapt to the site, conditions, uses, climate, surroundings, etc. before the result is built.

URBAN ALGORITHMS

» Non-trivial computation
» Procedure followed by the majority of buildings around the world, erected by their owners in informal settlements
» The "building industry" in wealthy societies represents only a very small portion of construction worldwide

TRADITIONAL URBAN DESIGN

» Uses human perception for both the footprints and positioning of buildings
» Computation is highly intuitive
» Alignment and relationship of each building to each other is complex and interactive

Traditional urban fabric

TRADITIONAL URBANISM IS NOT RANDOM!

» Decades of basic misunderstanding
» Traditional urban form is organized, complex, adaptive, but not random
» Proponents of non-computational urbanism recommend its replacement with simplistic non-computed forms

IRREDUCIBLE COMPLEXITY

» Evolved urban complexity is irreducible
» Irreducibly complex systems cannot be arrived at via a shortcut or formula
» Algorithmic description is as long as the algorithm required to produce them
» True of all biological systems

Today we understand much better how complex systems are generated from a very large number of steps. There is no simple formula for creating a complex system, although each of its many components is the result of some generative code. Learning from biological structure and from complex software systems, we know that simplistic urban forms are unsuitable human environments, but then so are artificially complex designs that have not evolved to adapt to human activities and physiology. Unfortunately, most planning today applies such non-adaptive forms uncritically, creating inhuman environments throughout the world. Often, the client (private or government agency) gives the job to a fashionable architect who has absolutely no idea of adaptive urban form, and instead creates a "sculpture" that people have to suffer for generations.

NON-COMPUTATIONAL DESIGN

» Monotonous repetition is not the result of computation
» Non-adaptive repeating modules could exist on any scale
» Much of post World-War II urban growth looks regular from the air
» Monofunctional residential zones

Typical plan of non-computed urbanism

The terrible misunderstanding of 20C urbanism was that traditional organic urban form is random (it's not), and had to be eliminated in the ideological interests of "rationality". In its place planners built monotonous repeating structures, the result of trivial computations that did not adapt to any human use and dimensions; did not adapt to the landscape, to local materials, to the climate, nor to anything else. An entirely separate tradition is represented by formal urbanism, which does indeed compute the plan of a city, but just as in the case of non-computed urban form, there is no feedback. Therefore, both non-computational design and non-interactive computational design are deficient as methods of building human-scale urban fabric.

NON-INTERACTIVE COMPUTATIONS

» Most mathematical algorithms are non-interactive — bad example
» This gives rise to rational attempts from some central planning authority
» "Ideal cities", "garden cities", "campuses"
» None of those have ever been successful in producing a living urban fabric

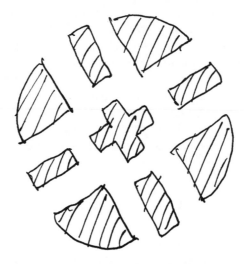

Non-interactive computation generates a formal
plan for an aggregate of buildings

A TOP-DOWN MIND-SET

» Top-down implementation
» "Formal" approach to planning looks more complex than non-computational
» But still fails for a human environment
» In social housing, non-adaptive geometry degrades social life

NON-ADAPTIVE COMPLEXITY

» No interaction or feedback in the algorithms used to compute "formal" urban schemes
» Their generated complexity works against living processes
» Computed forms do not adjust to human needs, paths, landscape, etc.

....

I believe that we are on the threshold of an entirely new understanding of urban form using a computational model. So far, the application of computation in design has been misused terribly, to generate monsters that are unadapted to human life. Christopher Alexander's paper "Harmony-Seeking Computations" together with my own paper "Urbanism as Computation" mark the beginnings of a fruitful direction for investigation. Most importantly, by casting urban design as adaptive computation, all the techniques developed elsewhere (in biology, mathematics, and computer science) can be brought in to help us design and reconstruct cities.

....

12.2. URBAN PLAZAS.

HEART OF NEIGHBORHOOD

» Project for Querétaro, Mexico
» Generative pattern for designing successful urban plazas
» INTENDED FOR THE NEW PARTS OF THE CITY
» City already has a sprawling 3-storey mixed-use urban fabric, but no community — it is fragmented

....

At this time, the difference in human quality between the historic center and the suburbs in Querétaro is like night and day, and much of this is due to the presence and quality of the urban plazas. My colleagues in Mexico and I are writing a generative code for successful urban plazas in the new parts of the city. Querétaro already has the appropriate density, and it is the morphology that has to be repaired through a catalytic geometry. Since pre-existing conditions are favorable, this can be achieved in part by inserting new urban plazas. Unfortunately, suburbia in the United States does not have the urban density to benefit immediately from such a reconstruction.

....

SOCIAL CAPITAL

» **Urban space is not merely the CONTAINER of social capital**
» **Urban space is ITSELF social capital**
» Social discourse occurs by connecting directly to other people
» — and indirectly by connecting to places, to nature, and thus to people

URBAN SPACE

» Patterns of human activity nearly always tie into urban space
» 20th-Century urbanism tried to internalize all urban space into the individual house and garden
» Frustrating quest for urban space that one individual or family controls

URBAN SPACE (CONT.)

» As a result, houses and lots have grown ever larger and larger
» Take over city for private living space
» Unsustainable, but is encouraged by developers and land speculators
» End of social capital in our society!

STRONG CONJECTURE

» N.A.S. and Alexis Hugh Ramírez
» "Can we reconnect fragmented urban fabric by inserting urban plazas?"
» Will new plazas act as catalysts to re-connect the rest of the city?
» Modernist urban plazas disconnect urban fabric — an observed fact

GENERATIVE CODE: PLAZAS - A

» Locate new square at intersection of intermediate-density roads
» Size of square follows historical type
» At least one edge touches on street
» At least one edge is pedestrian
» Build south-facing edge of square with porticoes, if appropriate to culture (where possible, do the west-facing side as well)

In most cases today, the space available for an urban plaza is immense when compared to the size of historical urban plazas. A plaza that is too large can be dysfunctional just as much as a plaza that is too small. This gigantism is due to the general loss of human scale in urban structure in the decades following World-War II. In those cases, we need to create two distinct, autonomous urban plazas that are sensitively connected so that they remain perceptually and functionally distinct.

GENERATIVE CODE: PLAZAS - B

- » Surrounded all around by buildings no more than 3 storeys high
- » No parking on or around plaza
- » Available parking behind, or under
- » Guarantee pedestrian feeding from at least 3 blocks all around plaza

GENERATIVE CODE: PLAZAS - C

- » Surrounding façades permeable to pedestrian — windows, doors, etc.
- » Very narrow street frontages only
- » Minimize use of modernist materials
- » No glass façades allowed
- » No sheer brick or concrete walls

GENERATIVE CODE: PLAZAS - D

- » All wall openings (doors, windows) must have a surround of width > 30cm
- » Use historical form language only
- » Ornamented façades and plaza itself
- » Use colors and natural materials
- » Signage in traditional lettering only

These considerations are not based upon aesthetics, but are biologically-motivated. It has been found that the information content of the buildings surrounding a plaza strongly influences the use of the plaza and its eventual success. The occupation and use of the plaza depends in an essential manner upon the architecture and visual effect of the surrounding region. It has to do with the informational and fractal qualities that affect us biologically. By sticking as much as possible to the historical form language, including a high degree of ornamentation, the correct information field is generated around the plaza.

GENERATIVE CODE: PLAZAS - E

- » Walk the ground to set footpaths
- » Save existing trees and landmarks
- » Design to include plants in the left-over spaces; abandon formal symmetry
- » Use traditional street furniture, highly ornamented down to < 5mm
- » No abstract sculptures or forms!

IMPORTANCE OF DETAIL

» Success of urban plaza is highly dependent on detail of structures
» Necessary but not sufficient condition is the presence of organized, coherent detail on the 3mm scale
» Can only be achieved by ornament
» ORNAMENT RULES PLAZA

PROPOSAL

» Project developed for the city government of Querétaro, Mexico
» Our generative code creates a new successful plaza every time
» We are not proposing a template
» Applied on the Federal level, we can create 5,000 urban plazas, all distinct

CHILDREN'S PLAYGROUNDS

» A plaza built according to our generative code is a playground
» Pedestrian access from surroundings
» Hopefully, the plaza will catalyze pedestrian urban life where none exists
» ACCESSIBLE green for children; opposite of today's "see but not touch"

12.3. DESIGNING FOR CHILDREN.

ANTI-CHILDREN CITIES

» Our children are negatively affected by today's built environment
» The geometry of urban landscape is hostile to children's sensibilities
» Most adults do not realize this — they are fooled by visual symbols

THE CHILDREN'S WORLD

» Experienced totally with senses
» Emotionally-based experiences
» Extremely sensitive to environment
» Child is not numbed like adults
» Is not yet conditioned to override emotions with abstract ideas

UNASKED QUESTIONS

» Can a child go out of a door and play safely in the environment?
» Can he/she explore without the parent fearing for its safety?
» How far can a child go anywhere on their own?

DOWNTOWNS

» Most downtowns in the US have been gutted of human scale
» Hostile glass or concrete fronts of skyscrapers are everywhere
» No permeability of street façades
» Hostile to both children and adults

SUBURBS — COMMERCIAL

» Effects are more subtle here
» Strip malls are pedestrian unfriendly
» The only pedestrian space is a short piece of sidewalk along stores
» No child can ever reach a store on foot from home, because those are designed for car access only

SUBURBS — RESIDENTIAL

» House surrounded by a yard is an impractical utopian image
» Front yard is too exposed for children to feel protected enough to play
» Back yard is a totally enclosed prison, and children feel this isolation

SUBURBS — RESIDENTIAL (CONT.)

» Suburban streets are built to the width and smoothness of a highway
» Danger grows exponentially with the street width! (documented accidents)
» Too dangerous for children to play on wide street in front of their house
» US cities do not allow rough paving that slows down cars in European cities

RESIDENTIAL SUBURBS BECOME UNINTENDED PARKING LOTS

» After a while, house garages are used as storage, filled with consumer junk
» Multiple family cars start taking over the street and driveways
» Suburb becomes a giant parking lot
» Goodbye to the promised "green garden" image of suburbia!

INTENTIONAL PARKING LOTS

» Giant open parking lots are terrifying and dangerous for children
» Feel threatened every second you are a pedestrian in the parking lot
» Most parking garages are not better — hostile prison-like environments

COMPLICITY OF PLANNERS

» Too dangerous for children to ride bicycles through neighborhood
» Planners refuse to change the codes to allow a genuinely child-friendly built environment
» Shockingly, adults have absolutely no idea of how to achieve this goal

SKYSCRAPERS AS PRISONS

» The most inhuman environment for children is the skyscraper
» Children lose all contact with nature and human reality
» This building typology isolates and diminishes the children's world to within one apartment or one room

FOUR-STOREY LIMIT

» Christopher Alexander already gave the criterion of a four-storey limit for apartment houses: PATTERN 21
» Based upon the distance children can successfully interact with their friends and parents on the ground
» Putting children into high-rises is a crime against humanity!

A NEW URBAN REALM

» Get rid of dangerous intersections, crossings, giant urban visual objects
» Get rid of prison-yard concrete playgrounds — a sadistic experiment
» Make entire urban space a playground
» Surround useless expanses of lawn by protecting structures to encourage play

WHY DID WE DO THIS?

» Why are Western cities so totally, obsessively, child-unfriendly?
» Because modernist design is based on an inhuman vision of people who did not care for children
» Ideology overrides human life, even ignores the future of the human race!

CHRISTOPHER DAY

» Already wrote a book on design with children in mind
» "Environment and Children: Passive Lessons from the Everyday Environment", Architectural Press/Elsevier, Oxford, 2007

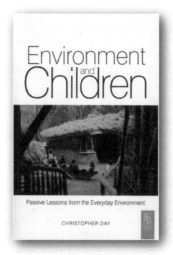

„Environment and Children"

FAVELAS AS EXAMPLES

» We are too arrogant, too caught up with ridiculous and destructive ideas of modernity, too dependent upon mechanization, too proud to admit we have destroyed our cities
» We are too proud to learn from poor people who have a better urban sense that we do!

12.4. FAVELAS AND SOCIAL HOUSING.

A LARGE PART OF HUMANITY

» 1 billion people live in favelas
» The majority of those regions have unhealthy living conditions
» The physical structures are made from unhealthy or unstable materials
» BUT THE FORM IS ORGANIC, AND GENERATES URBAN LIFE!

THE PRESUMED SOLUTION

» Every government wants to replace favelas with industrial housing
» The intention is to visually clean up their urban structure
» The government incorrectly assumes that the people want an ordered environment above all else

NO SOLUTION TO DRASTIC PROBLEM

» The system responsible for erecting industrial social housing can never solve the problem
» There are too many people
» There is not enough money
» Inhabitants of industrial housing hate their houses — they find them alien

A NEW PROPOSAL

» "Favelas and Social Housing: An Urbanism of Self-Organization"
» Paper by N.A.S., David Brain, Andrés Duany, Michael Mehaffy, & Ernesto Philibert-Petit
» Based in large part on the earlier work of Christopher Alexander

OUR CRITERIA FOR SUCCESS

» We consider a housing project successful if it is LOVED by its residents
» … unsuccessful if it is despised by its residents
» EMOTIONS ARE CONSEQUENCES OF THE CONNECTIVE GEOMETRY!

THE KEY TO SUCCESS

» Utilize and harness the processes of self-organization
» Cultivate the connection between physical and social complexity
» Reverse machine typologies for social housing practiced during past century
» Abandon the ideology of modernism

ECOSYSTEM COMPETITION

» Favelas are self-built, and lie outside government control
» Social housing blocks are built by government to impose its control
» Conflict between the two models wastes useful resources and does not solve the housing problem

ARTIFICIAL VERSUS ORGANIC

» Housing blocks versus Favelas
» Usually artificial versus An organic growth
» Planned housing versus Not formally planned
» Imposition of human will versus Extensions of human biology
» Typical top-down process versus Typical bottom-up processes

GENERATIVE CODE FOR OWNER-BUILT SOCIAL HOUSING

» **10 steps to build a new community**
» Government provides materials
» We (NGO advisors) provide advice
» Future residents provide the labor, or at least assist with labor
» Government provides the minimal infrastructure

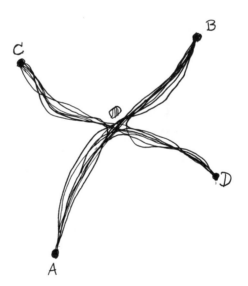

1. Walk the ground to define paths: main street A-B and cross street C-D, whose layout is determined by the topography and surrounding transportation network.

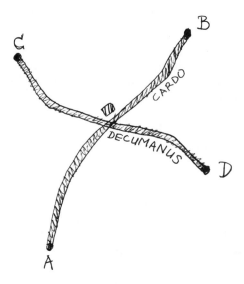

2. Cardo and decumanus (the principal and cross streets in Roman town planning) define main streets.

3. Urban spaces chosen by emotional feedback, become bubbles in street structure.

*NOTE ON URBAN SPACES

» Save existing pieces of nature: trees, rocks within urban space
» Save any features that can establish common interest
» In older societies, urban space contained sacred elements
» Urban space defined "sacred space"

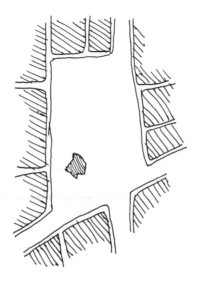

4. Urban square defined by surrounding buildings — no setbacks.

A lesson from this procedure, as illustrated in Figure 4, is that the town square doesn't have to be square. In fact, only in rare occasions should a town square actually be square or symmetric. This is seen repeatedly in historical urban plazas that have evolved over time. If we build a new city by following adaptive rules, then we need to allow for the possibility that the town square is shaped by the flows and the evolution of the surrounding urban fabric, and not to impose a rigid symmetrical plan.

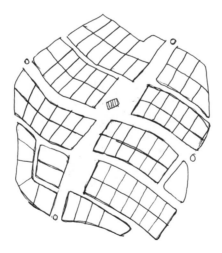

5. Space between lots defines the streets, not the other way around. Mixed urban fabric fills the plan, leaving left-over space for streets.

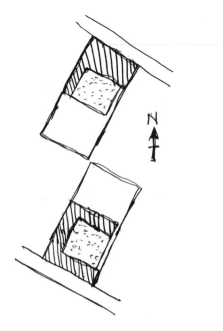

6. Patios surrounding house are oriented to catch the sun.

*NOTE ON THE BUILDINGS

» We don't offer a standardized plan
» Future residents work with a flexible, recommended plan that is adjusted, and only then is the lot measured
» There is a margin for change to adapt to each family's individual needs

The usual criticism of "loss of freedom" because of individualization is false. An individually adapted house for a particular family serves just as well for a new future resident. Once built by following an adapted process, a structure leaves its imprint of "humanity" that is recognized by all future residents. They can make changes if they wish. Christopher Alexander's students have done an enormous amount of research verifying this point. It is only the non-adapted industrial typology with a standardized plan that is equally unloved by any resident that will occupy it. Look at Stewart Brand's book "How Buildings Learn", Penguin, New York, 1995.

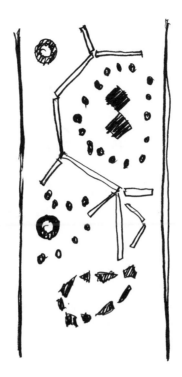

7. Residents design a pattern on their sidewalk, with an example here seen in plan, while the concrete is still fresh.

*NOTE ON THE SIDEWALKS

» First part of entire project to be built
» Each family will truly own their portion of sidewalk, because they ornament it with tiles, pebbles, etc.
» "We made it, therefore it's ours"
» Establishes the deepest sense of belonging to the residents

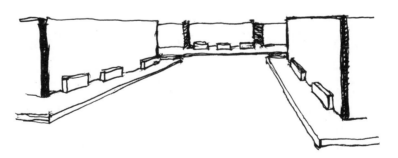

8. Façades, sidewalks, and benches reinforce urban space.

9. Wide, thick boundary defines entry as process of transition.

Entry *as a process of transition goes back to Alexander's Patterns 112: ENTRANCE TRANSITION, and 225: FRAMES AS THICKENED EDGES. This is so important for all buildings, not only in self-built housing, but it has been suppressed by modernist ideologues who like to have entrances punched as holes in a wall. This does violence to both the materials and to the wall's geometry, reminding us of tears in a woven fabric, or of bullet holes.*

10. Provide materials so that each owner ornaments their own dwelling.

THE KEY TO CONSTRUCTING LIVING URBAN FABRIC

» Combines the bottom-up favela with top-down social housing
» The cheapest solution!
» Only slightly more expensive than building favelas (which are free)
» It is also the best for the long-term

OBSTACLES TO OUR SOLUTION!

» The myth of large numbers is antiquated thinking
» Control of design and manufacture assumes standardized templates
» Standard social housing model conforms to industrial image of mass-production of the 1920s

FALSE PARADIGM

» The ONLY reason for standard production of housing is administrative control, NOT quality of product
» Identical, mass-produced units are easier for accounting purposes
» Government bureaucrats care more to maintain their bureaucratic system

THREAT TO GOVERNMENT?

» A government feels threatened by the ORGANIC GEOMETRY of the favela, more than by anything else
» So… government prefers to subsidize the large construction companies
» Desire to impose control prevents a viable solution to housing crisis

WISE GOVERNMENT DECISION

» We must build mixed-use CITY, not cheap dormitories
» We build for living beings, not to cram the maximum number of people into the largest boxes
» Have to get industrial contractors out of controlling social housing

OBSTACLE FROM BUILDERS

» Industry prefers to build modernist block housing, and not bother with people's wishes — it's simpler
» Lucrative sales of blocks, and government pays for modules
» But builders can still make a profit from our individualized method!

ARCHITECTS HAVE IT WRONG

» Architects' idea of "good" design has nothing to do with human feelings
» They rely on abstract concepts of design and form
» Architect-designed social housing is oppressive and inhuman

POLITICAL OPPOSITION

» From the Left: "everyone is equal, so they must have identical houses"
» From the Right: "poor people have no right to personalized dwellings"
» From the Center: bureaucracy takes care of social housing, which must impose industrial uniformity for pragmatic reasons

OBSTACLE FROM RESIDENTS

» Poor people have seen images on TV
» … of unsustainable American houses
» They want the same thing!
» Don't know that their own tradition provides more sustainable patterns, or even why that is important
» Don't know that they will probably be forced into concrete prison boxes

THE GEOMETRY OF CONTROL

» Not only social life becomes a victim of geometrical control
» Trees and natural features are all eliminated because they are "dirty": they are inconvenient to deal with and their complexity ruins the ideological "purity" of hard plazas so beloved by modernist architects and planners
» The industrial landscape is lifeless
» Life and living urban geometry are complex, not simplistic

NEW ROLE FOR NATURE

» Nowadays, nature is a threat to modernist geometry, and is only partially re-introduced as a purely decorative element
» Wholeness of site is destroyed
» We must retain, protect, and privilege nature to create a living environment

PLACES OF SIGNIFICANCE

» Sacred spaces — places we love
» Places of community
» They exist in traditional urban fabric, but not in any of today's developments
» We have lost the sense of the sacred
» We have lost the public places we can attach to emotionally

CONCLUSION

» Favelas and social housing can be amalgamated into a single hybrid housing process

» Self-construction, with government support and expert advice (from us)
» We see this as the ONLY solution to a major problem facing humanity

CONCLUSION: THE END OF MYSTIFICATION.

We — a group of architects, urbanists, and sociologists — have the rules that can be used to create a new city on the human scale. We are also ready to reconstruct the suburbs and inhuman urban peripheries in order to generate living urban fabric. These rules are developed out of science and mathematics. Although we have published them freely in articles, books, videos, and on the World-Wide Web, these rules are unknown and are ignored by the "big name" architects put in charge of constructing and upgrading our cities today. As those individuals are only playing for power, they do not care about scientific developments, unless it is to misuse scientific terms like "fractals" and "chaos" in dishonest and erroneous ways to promote their monstrous projects.

My book is a manifesto against the twisting of human nature. During the past few decades, society has lost a fundamental right: the freedom to choose the character of our living environment, which is a coup d'état against democracy itself. Everywhere, buildings and monstrous structures are imposed upon us, with their alien and inhuman surfaces, while human-scale urban fabric is destroyed and replaced by alien structures, giant parking lots, and freeways that cut through the city center. Social experiments are implemented on a massive scale, treating people as if they were toys. At the same time, all of this has been presented as some marvelous "progress", often with a political mask of presumed liberation. In the final analysis, it is only a vast propaganda.

The fundamental essence of life resides in the production of information. Every living being is a complex system of information, one part of it residing in the genetic material, and in human beings, another part stored as a body of knowledge. This stored "memory" is deposited in our cultural, technical, scientific and artistic knowledge, etc. Architecture is also a storehouse of information discovered and developed through the centuries by every culture. The International Style lost all of this knowledge, and today the self-proclaimed architectural avant-gardes continue to despise inherited information. My group of friends and collaborators has developed and re-discovered laws for an architecture on the human scale, which we have published openly on the Internet. The movements of contemporary architecture, by contrast, practice mystification, claiming that it is necessary to choose a famous architect in order to design any "important" building. They claim that such fashionable high-profile architects have secret knowledge that allows them to produce an innovative design. Mystification destroys open information for all, as it destroys freedom of choice.

Contemporary science is the most democratic system in existence, allowing a free criticism of its results. It is not founded solely on the authority of any particular individual, but represents a combination of the collective work of generations of people. I am member of the "open-source" movement and of peer-to-peer urbanism, and the notion that a so-called "expert" from the avant-garde somehow possesses secret and hidden knowledge about design strikes me as fundamentally anti-democratic. Useful information must be verifiable; that is, open to all who wish to verify it and apply it, and not kept hidden like a pseudo-religious secret that has become dogma. This is the way that scientific knowledge advances itself and rejects obscurantism. Today's avant-garde is none other than an obscurantist movement. Why all of this steel, glass, and concrete in fashionable buildings yet not a trace of harmonious ornament? Why all these empty, twisted, and unbalanced forms? No scientific explanation is ever offered, because none exists. We are given only ideological propaganda.

It was my group of friends who developed fundamental new results to plan urban fabric: concepts like fractal loading; the network city; universal scaling and hierarchy; generative codes; archetypes; urban coherence; form languages; city microsurgery, and so on. The self-proclaimed avant-garde ignores all of this. And then, the famous architects don't care at all for the majority of construction activity on the earth: the self-building of favelas, the problem of social housing, the urban periphery, the growing shantytowns of the world, the frightening consumption of agricultural areas by urban sprawl. Far away from obscenely expensive fashionable buildings, humanity constructs in order to survive. Only when they see the opportunity to make a profit, the "name" architects propose pharaonic projects without understanding anything about the needs of humans as individuals. The "name" architects never take the time to learn about human biology and sociology.

We, by contrast, work constantly on these problems. We are developing techniques of participative design and planning that will enable us to save the urban peripheries, and to restructure informal housing in order to generate a truly human environment.

In every country we can find several traditions of sustainable building and planning tied to the human scale. There is no exception: every country and every people have developed more than one architectural tradition with the measure of the human being, because that is human nature. The architecture of the human scale is an extension of our Biology. My friends and I have shown that evolved architectural rules have the same source as do physical and biological rules. It was only with industrialization that we lost this fundamental link between Biology and Architecture. Today we have forgotten all of this in a fatal amnesia. Design languages and traditions have been rejected by the Modernist movement — the International Style — to the point where we are no longer able to recognize the existing architectural wealth around the world.

One must search again within modest architectural traditions, in the architecture forgotten by the glossy magazines, looking not only at vernacular and historical architectures but also to self-building: the architecture of the favelas all over the world. Outside the fashionable world where a style is imposed because it is "approved by the international intelligentsia", human beings build according to their body and their heart. They make the best they can do with available materials to construct a living environment in which to live and be with their family.

It is astonishing how all the architectonic traditions of the entire world have been buried by today's avant-garde, even if those traditions are still practiced in front of our very eyes! The negative propaganda is so effective that it does not allow architects (nor the majority of the population) to perceive and to value their own building culture. People do not see this because someone from the elite has proclaimed their architectural tradition to be a sign of "decadence", a "retrograde" practice, and to therefore stand as an impediment to the hyper-technological development promised by the class of global consumerist elites. A monumental swindle!

CREDITS

TEXTS REFERRED TO:

I refer to the monograph "Harmony-seeking computations" by Christopher Alexander, International Journal of Unconventional Computing, (to appear), draft available from <www.livingneighborhoods.org/library/harmony-seeking-computations.pdf>. I also use Alexander's "The Nature of Order", Books 1, 2, 3, and 4, and Stephen Wolfram's "A New Kind of Science".

LECTURES GIVEN OVER TWELVE WEEKS IN THE SPRING OF 2008.

Each one-hour lecture was repeated twice a week. The first time around, it was offered at Michael G. Imber Architects, 111 W. El Prado St., San Antonio, Texas 78212. The same lecture was repeated at The University of Texas at San Antonio, One UTSA Circle, San Antonio, Texas 78249. The second lecture was transmitted via videoconference from the University Distance Learning Center to participating institutions throughout the world.

ACKNOWLEDGMENT:

My thanks to Michael D. Imbimbo for a thorough reading of the lecture notes and for many useful suggestions. I am extremely grateful to Dr. George Perry, Dean of the College of Sciences and Professor of Biology at the University of Texas at San Antonio, for supporting this project. He kindly gave me time to prepare and deliver the lecture series in the Spring of 2008, and then additional time to prepare the book in the Fall of 2009.

ADDITIONAL CREDITS:

Three new sections were added to this book. Sections 1.4 and 1.5 are from a lecture presented to the Architecture School of the University of Texas at San Antonio and to Michael Imber Architects in February and March of 2009. Section 12.1 comes from a lecture presented at the University of Delft, Holland in September of 2009.

Alexandros A. Lavdas PhD (a neurobiologist) and George Papanikolaou MD PhD (a geneticist) are Athenians, like myself, and are working in basic research and in the biotechnology industry, respectively. As scientists interested in the structural relations between complexity in the built environment and natural complexity, they graciously accepted to write the two introductory essays.

Alexandros is Researcher Grade C (Assistant Professor) at the Hellenic Pasteur Institute, and George holds a managerial position in the Pharmaceutical industry.

When I asked my editor Harald Gottfried if I should get an introduction by a famous contemporary architect (either one of my friends, or even someone in the opposite camp who might be persuaded to do it as a friendly gesture), he answered: "I'd prefer to have people read the book without prejudice, not saying it is a result of very narrow concerns because architect *** wrote the introduction. If scientifically justified results of your interdisciplinary research concerning architecture lead to conclusions that prove a certain kind of architecture, at least different if not contrary to modernism, high-tech, blobitecture, gadgetecture, ... to be right, then I think it should be presented as what it is: Science. Any introduction that's influenced by particular preferences for a certain flavor of architecture will ruin the neutral, scientific attempt." So I asked two brilliant scientists.

The book's conclusion is a translation of part of an interview published in Italian in the national newspaper La Repubblica on 23 November 2009.

FIGURES

Unless otherwise noted, I drew all the sketches and diagrams. The two sets of Leitner Diagrams in Sections 5.2 and 6.1 were drawn by Helmut Leitner, and the figures of the Schooner Bay Project in Section 11.3 were drawn by Stephen Mouzon. I am grateful for their permission to publish these diagrams, and they appear in this book for the first time. The drawing in section 11.2 (page 209) is by Léon Krier. It has appeared at various times, for example in Demetri Porphyrios, Editor, "Leon Krier: Houses, Palaces, Cities", Academy Publications, London, 1984, pages 70-71. Figure on page 160 is adapted from the cover of "Poesie sur Alger" by Le Corbusier, Falaize, Paris, 1950.. Original cover art © Fondation Le Corbusier/Artists Rights Society, 2007.

embryonic development 29
emergence 81-82, 108, 149
emergent systems 82, 103, 108-109, 149
emotional regeneration 28, 63
entropy 125, 127
entry as a process of transition 240
Environment and Children 233
evolution of artefacts 144
evolutionary regression 143-146
exponential sequence 20

Fathy, Hassan 86
Favelas 199-200, 234-235
Fibonacci sequence 18
Fifteen Fundamental Properties 115-124
Five steps for regeneration 195
folding 44-48
fonts 144-145
form follows purpose 144
form language 29, 85, 135, 140-142, 178, 229-230
form-based codes 189, 204, 207-208
formal design 85, 226-227
four-storey limit 232
fractal castle 39
fractal dimension 60, 64-67
fractal windows 65-67
fractals 37-47, 58-60, 66-69, 81-82, 97, 122
frames 26, 240
functional typology 140-141

Garden Cities 226
generative codes 84, 189-190, 196, 223-225
genetic algorithms 136-137, 196
geometric recursion 37
geometry of control 242
Giraudoux, Jean 159
Glide reflection 170-172
Golden Mean 23
Golden Rectangle 19
Good shape 119
good tall buildings 219
Gradients 121
Grameen Bank 73, 195
Grameen model for repair 193
grouping 31-34

Haas, Tigran 190-191
harmony-seeking process 107-108
healing, post-operative 64
Heerwagen, Judith 153
high-level description 107
higher dimensions 88

Hillis, Danny 136-137
humans become more machine-like 151
Hypercharge 88, 180-181
hyperspace 86-88
hyperspace 87-90

Imber, Michael 247
Imbimbo, Michael 247
implicit axis 49, 170-171
implied center 99
incompleteness theorem 104
incomprehensible complexity 136
industrialization 42, 152-154, 202
inhuman design 156, 157, 161-162, 164-165, 194-196, 218, 225, 232, 242
inhuman experiments 152, 155-156, 160-163
inhuman urban codes 189, 196, 203-204, 232
initial condition 79-80, 85, 104
Intelligence-Based Design 166
interior/exterior dimensions 90
inverse-power law 57
Isospin 88, 125, 180-183

Joye, Jannick 28

Kellert, Stephen 153
Kolmogorov complexity 31
Krier, Léon 209
Kunstler, James Howard 203

Lack of ornament 62
land clearance 194
Laplante, Martin 69
latent center 99
Lavdas, Alexandros 7, 247
Le Corbusier 30, 51-53, 151, 156-160, 173, 203, 218-219, 233
Le Corbusier's dog "Pinceau" 159
legalizing codes 203
Leitner diagrams, first set 102-103
Leitner diagrams, second set 116-123
Leitner, Helmut 102-103, 116-123
Léon Krier's pie 209
Levels of scale 117
life of the site 190-191
linking small and large scales 126
Local symmetries 119
love and ownership 189

Machines become more human 151
Mador, Martin 153